Fast Food

Fast Food

Over 80 recipes,
ready in 30
minutes or less

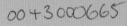

hamlyn

A Pyramid Paperback

First published in Great Britain in 2006 by Hamlyn,
a division of Octopus Publishing Group Ltd,
2–4 Heron Quays, London E14 4JP

ISBN-13: 978-0-600-61457-9
ISBN-10: 0-600-61457-3

A CIP catalogue record for this book is available
from the British Library

Printed and bound in China

10 9 8 7 6 5 4 3 2 1

Notes

Both metric and imperial measurements have
been given in all recipes. Use one set of
measurements only, and not a mixture of both.

Meat and poultry should be cooked thoroughly.
To test if poultry is cooked, pierce the flesh
through the thickest part with a skewer or fork –
the juices should run clear, never pink or red.

This book includes dishes made with nuts and
nut derivatives. It is advisable for those with
known allergic reactions to nuts and nut
derivatives and those who may be potentially
vulnerable to these allergies, such as pregnant
and nursing mothers, invalids, the elderly, babies
and children, to avoid dishes made with nuts and
nut oils. It is also prudent to check the labels of
pre-prepared ingredients for the possible
inclusion of nut derivatives.

The Department of Health advises that eggs
should not be consumed raw. This book contains
some dishes made with raw or lightly cooked eggs.
It is prudent for more vulnerable people, such as
pregnant and nursing mothers, invalids, the elderly,
babies and young children, to avoid uncooked or
lightly cooked dishes made with eggs.

Contents

Introduction

You want a tasty, satisfying meal, but you don't have the time to spend hours slaving in the kitchen. Well, forget supermarket ready meals and convenience foods – here are over 75 recipe ideas, all prepared and cooked in about 30 minutes, and some in considerably less. Each recipe gives the preparation and cooking times, and there are lots of fast food tips to help you along the way.

THE RECIPES

Whether you're cooking for yourself, the two of you, your family or friends, you want no-fuss food that's easy to prepare, looks impressive, smells enticing and, most importantly, tastes delicious. These fast food ideas include great recipes for meat, poultry and fish, as well as for soups, starters, vegetables and desserts.

Homemade soups not only taste better than ready-prepared ones, they're much cheaper and you know exactly what has gone into them. Fast food soups feature hot and spicy, fresh and creamy and filling and chunky varieties – just add some good bread and you've a nourishing, quick meal.

Eggs provide wonderfully fast meals – try the Herby Eggs with Smoked Salmon on page 21, or the Sage and Goats' Cheese Frittata on page 24, both prepared and cooked in about 15 minutes.

Boneless poultry breasts are the ideal fast food, as they cook in just a few minutes and can be adapted to whatever cuisine you fancy – be it Thai, Japanese, Italian, Mexican or Chinese.

Fish, too, is a brilliant fast food, whether whole, such as mackerel, or in steaks and fillets – quick cooking is the key to success here. Seafood, such as prawns, squid and scallops, also needs just the briefest of cooking time.

Quick-cooking meats include fillets, chops and liver, pan-fried, grilled or roasted, and minced meat such as the beef in the Red-hot Hamburgers on page 55 – no additives, just pure meat.

FAST FOOD INGREDIENTS

The key to good food is good-quality ingredients, and this is especially so with fast food. If you are able, buy the best-quality meat, chicken or fish you can find. Use seasonal fruits and vegetables – they'll not only taste better, but they'll be cheaper, too, and the ready-washed salads and vegetables will help you cut corners and save you time and energy.

Grow a few herbs on the windowsill such as parsley, chives, coriander, mint or whatever you fancy – they'll come in handy for adding that extra-special flavour to your cooked dish.

Fruit is healthy, nutritious, naturally sweet and delicious, and it features a lot in the Desserts chapter. Try the luscious hot figs smothered with honeyed yogurt and ready in just 15 minutes on page 116, or the Drunken Orange Slices on page 118 – juicy slices of caramelized orange topped with a Cointreau-flavoured syrup.

GETTING ORGANIZED

It's really worth getting organized and having a well-stocked store cupboard, so that you always have the basics for your meals and, if necessary, need only pick up a few fresh ingredients on your way home. For example, if you have some good olive oil, a can of good-quality tomatoes and a packet of pasta, you can whip up a tasty meal in the time it takes to cook the pasta. Anything added is a bonus, but the emphasis is on quality. So spend some time once in a while on stocking up your store cupboard – see the box below for some suggested staples.

THE FAST FOOD STORE CUPBOARD
- **Oils** Such as olive oil, sunflower oil, vegetable oil, groundnut oil, sesame oil
- **Vinegars** Such as red and white wine, tarragon and balsamic
- **Mustards**
- **Canned foods** Such as tomatoes, beans, lentils, anchovies, tuna, salmon, sardines, coconut milk, olives, black cherries
- **Ground herbs and spices**: buy in small quantities and replenish regularly
- **Dry goods** Such as pasta, noodles, rice, polenta and instant couscous
- **Nuts, seeds, desiccated coconut, creamed coconut**
- **Ready-made curry pastes and chilli sauces**
- **Bottled foods** Such as lemon juice, passata (sieved tomatoes), pesto, tomato paste, sun-blush tomatoes, peppers and capers
- **Sauces and condiments** Such as Thai fish sauce, soy sauce, hoisin sauce and Worcestershire sauce
- **Pickles and chutneys**
- **Vacuum-packed beetroot in natural juices**
- **Ready-to-eat dried fruit**
- **Honey and maple syrup**
- **Gelatine**
- **Sweet biscuits** Such as amaretti
- **Ready-made meringue nests**

Plus the everyday staples such as flour, sugar, salt, etc.

Store onions and potatoes in a cool, dark place – they'll last much longer that way.

THE FAST FOOD FREEZER
Keep some of the following in the freezer – they'll make life easier when you're trying to whip up a meal in half an hour:
- **Frozen peas**
- **Prawns**
- **Bread** – keep some baguette, ciabatta and focaccia in the freezer as well as other good breads
- **Berry fruits**
- **Filo pastry**
- **Vanilla ice cream**

Homemade ice creams and granitas are always appreciated. Use a wet weekend to make some in advance, ready to be whipped out of the freezer and served when you need a refreshing dessert, such as the Lemon Yogurt Ice on page 110.

ALCOHOL

It's always good to have a few bottles in the cupboard or the refrigerator to use in your cooking – useful ones include dry and cream sherry, dry white wine, red wine, Marsala, Cointreau, sake, whisky and lager.

MARINATING

Some of the recipes call for ingredients to be marinated if possible – use this time as breathing space to prepare the rest of the ingredients, lay the table or have a glass of wine. Where a longer marinade is called for, prepare that step the night before or first thing in the morning.

FAST FOOD TIPS

• **Keep things simple** – focus on fresh, natural tastes.

• **Keep your store cupboard** and freezer stocked up.

• **Buy the best-quality food you can afford** – and that goes for the items you choose for your store cupboard, too.

• **Buy ready-washed salad leaves** and ready-prepared vegetables, to help cut down on preparation time.

• **Get the fishmonger or butcher** to do any necessary work, such as scaling, filleting or boning fish and meat.

• **Use spare time** to make chicken or vegetable stock and ice creams and granitas to store in the freezer.

• **Preheat your grill or oven** while you're preparing the ingredients, then it will be ready as soon as you are.

• **Boil water in the kettle for pasta** – it will be quicker than in a pan.

Soups and Starters

Light and fragrant, rich and spicy or fruity and herby, these fabulous soups score high on flavour and nutrients yet low on time and work. As do the elegant starters – deliciously filled parcels, savoury-topped toasts and crispy cheese morsels.

serves **4**
preparation time **10 minutes**
cooking time **10 minutes**

Thai prawn broth

1.2 litres (2 pints) vegetable stock
2 teaspoons Thai red curry paste
4 dried kaffir lime leaves, torn into pieces
4 teaspoons Thai fish sauce
2 spring onions, trimmed and sliced
150 g (5 oz) shiitake mushrooms, sliced
125 g (4 oz) soba (Japanese noodles)
½ red pepper, cored, deseeded and diced
125 g (4 oz) pak choi, thinly sliced
250 g (8 oz) frozen cooked peeled prawns, thawed and rinsed
1 small bunch of fresh coriander leaves, torn into pieces

1 Pour the stock into a saucepan and add the curry paste, lime leaves, fish sauce, spring onions and mushrooms. Bring to the boil, then reduce the heat and simmer for 5 minutes.

2 Bring a separate saucepan of water to the boil, add the soba and cook for 3 minutes.

3 Meanwhile, add all the remaining ingredients to the broth and cook for 2 minutes until piping hot.

4 Drain the noodles, rinse with fresh hot water and spoon into the base of 4 bowls. Ladle the hot prawn broth over the top and serve immediately.

FAST FOOD TIP
To turn this into a vegetarian broth, simply leave out the prawns and fish sauce.

serves **4**
preparation time **10 minutes**
cooking time **10 minutes**

Hot and sour soup

1.3 litres (2¼ pints) fish stock
4 dried kaffir lime leaves
4 slices of peeled fresh root
ginger
1 red chilli, deseeded and
sliced
1 lemon grass stalk
125 g (4 oz) mushrooms,
sliced
100 g (3½ oz) rice noodles
75 g (3 oz) baby spinach
leaves
125 g (4 oz) cooked peeled
tiger prawns
2 tablespoons lemon juice
freshly ground black pepper

1 Put the stock, lime leaves, ginger, chilli and lemon grass into a large saucepan, cover and bring to the boil. Add the mushrooms, reduce the heat and simmer for 2 minutes. Break the noodles into short lengths, drop into the soup and simmer for 3 minutes.

2 Add the spinach and prawns and simmer for 2 minutes until the prawns are heated through.

3 Add the lemon juice, then remove and discard the lemon grass stalk and season with pepper before serving.

serves **4**
preparation time **10 minutes**
cooking time **20 minutes**

Fresh tomato
and almond soup

**1 kg (2 lb) vine-ripened
   tomatoes, roughly chopped**
2 garlic cloves, crushed
**300 ml (½ pint) vegetable
   stock**
**2 tablespoons extra virgin
   olive oil**
1 teaspoon caster sugar
**100 g (3½ oz) ground almonds,
   toasted**
**salt and freshly ground black
   pepper**

basil oil
**150 ml (¼ pint) extra virgin
   olive oil**
15 g (½ oz) basil leaves

1 Put the tomatoes into a saucepan with the garlic, stock, oil and sugar, and season with salt and pepper. Bring to the boil, then reduce the heat and simmer gently for 15 minutes.

2 Meanwhile, prepare the basil oil. Pour the oil into a blender or food processor, add the basil and a pinch of salt and whiz to a smooth purée. Alternatively, pound the oil, basil and salt together using a pestle and mortar. Transfer to a bottle or bowl and set aside.

3 Stir the almonds into the soup and heat to warm it through, then serve in warmed bowls, drizzled with the basil oil.

FAST FOOD TIP
Make this soup during the summer months when tomatoes are at their juiciest and best. The addition of ground almonds not only flavours the soup but also helps to thicken it. To toast the almonds, dry-fry them in a frying pan over a medium heat, stirring constantly until golden brown.

serves **4**
preparation time **10 minutes**
cooking time **30 minutes**

Chunky chorizo, pasta
and bean soup

4 tablespoons extra virgin
   olive oil
1 large onion, chopped
50 g (2 oz) chorizo sausage,
   chopped
4 garlic cloves, crushed
2 tablespoons chopped thyme
750 ml (1¼ pints) chicken
   stock
1.2 litres (2 pints) passata
   (sieved tomatoes)
2 x 400 g (13 oz) cans borlotti
   beans, drained and rinsed
200 g (7 oz) small pasta
   shapes, such as
   conchigliette
3 tablespoons chopped basil
salt and freshly ground black
   pepper
freshly grated Parmesan
   cheese, to serve

1 Heat the oil in a saucepan and fry the onion, chorizo, garlic and thyme for 5 minutes. Meanwhile, heat the stock in a separate saucepan.

2 Add the hot stock, passata, beans and salt and pepper to the onion mixture and bring to the boil. Reduce the heat, cover and simmer for 15 minutes.

3 Stir in the pasta and basil and cook for a further 8–10 minutes until the pasta is tender. Adjust the seasoning if necessary, then spoon into warmed bowls and serve topped with grated Parmesan.

FAST FOOD TIP
The tiny pasta shapes used for soup are known as pastina; there are hundreds of different varieties to choose from – use any type you like.

serves **4**
preparation time **10 minutes**
cooking time **30 minutes**

Curried vegetable soup

40 g (1½ oz) ghee or butter
1 onion, chopped
2 garlic cloves, crushed
2 teaspoons grated fresh root
  ginger
1 large potato, diced
1 large carrot, diced
600 ml (1 pint) vegetable
  stock
2 teaspoons ground
  coriander
1 teaspoon ground cumin
½ teaspoon garam masala
125 g (4 oz) red lentils
600 ml (1 pint) tomato juice
salt and freshly ground black
  pepper

to serve
raita
naan bread

1 Melt the ghee or butter in a saucepan and fry the onion, garlic, ginger, potato and carrot for 10 minutes. Meanwhile, heat the stock in a separate saucepan.

2 Add the hot stock to the onion mixture, then stir in the spices and add the remaining ingredients. Bring to the boil, then reduce the heat, cover and simmer for 20 minutes until the lentils and vegetables are cooked.

3 Adjust the seasoning, then spoon into warmed bowls. Top each bowl with some raita and serve with naan bread.

FAST FOOD TIP
Ghee is similar to clarified butter and is traditionally used in India for shallow-frying. You can often find ghee in cans in larger supermarkets or purchase it from a specialist Indian food store.

serves **4**
preparation time **10 minutes, plus standing**
cooking time **15–20 minutes**

Parmesan and herb polenta wedges
with spicy cherry tomato salsa

450 ml (¾ pint) water
125 g (4 oz) instant polenta
   or cornmeal
75 g (3 oz) butter
75 g (3 oz) freshly grated
   Parmesan cheese
2 tablespoons chopped chives
2 tablespoons roughly
   chopped parsley
2 tablespoons chopped
   chervil
salt and freshly ground black
   pepper

spicy cherry tomato salsa
300 g (10 oz) ripe cherry
   tomatoes, quartered
2 small red chillies, deseeded
   and finely chopped
1 small red onion, finely
   chopped
2 tablespoons chilli oil
2 tablespoons olive oil
2 tablespoons lime juice
2 tablespoons shredded mint

1 Heat the water in a saucepan until simmering, then pour in the polenta or cornmeal and beat well with a wooden spoon until it is thick and smooth. Reduce the heat and continue stirring for about 5 minutes (or according to the packet instructions) until cooked.

2 Remove the pan from the heat, add the butter, Parmesan and herbs and stir until well combined. Season with salt and pepper, then turn into a greased 25 cm (10 inch) pizza or cake tin, at least 2.5 cm (1 inch) deep. Smooth the top with the back of a spoon and leave to set for 5–10 minutes.

3 Meanwhile, combine all the salsa ingredients in a bowl and season with salt and pepper. Set aside.

4 Carefully remove the set polenta from the pan, transfer it to a chopping board and cut into 8 wedges.

5 Heat a ridged griddle pan over a high heat. Put the polenta wedges into the pan and cook for 2–3 minutes on each side until heated through and golden. Serve 2 wedges per person with a spoonful of the salsa on the side.

serves **4**
preparation time **10 minutes**
cooking time **4 minutes**

Crispy Parma ham parcels
with blue cheese and pears

8 slices of Parma ham or prosciutto
100 g (3½ oz) creamy blue cheese, such as Roquefort, Saint Agur, dolcelatte or Gorgonzola, cut into thin slices
1 teaspoon thyme leaves
1 pear, peeled, cored and diced
25 g (1 oz) shelled walnuts, chopped

to serve
watercress tossed in olive oil and balsamic vinegar
1 pear, peeled, quartered, cored and sliced

1 Place a slice of Parma ham or prosciutto on a chopping board, then put a second slice across it to form a cross shape. Arrange one-quarter of the cheese slices in the centre, scatter with some thyme, then top with some of the diced pear. Add a few walnuts, then fold over the sides of the ham to form a neat parcel. Repeat to make 4 parcels.

2 Heat a ridged griddle pan over a medium heat. Put the parcels into the pan and cook for about 2 minutes on each side until the ham is crisp and the cheese is beginning to ooze out of the sides. Alternatively, cook under a preheated medium-hot grill.

3 Serve the parcels immediately with the dressed watercress leaves and slices of pear.

serves **2**
preparation time **5 minutes**
cooking time **3 minutes**

Herby eggs
with smoked salmon

150 g (5 oz) silken tofu
3 eggs
15 g (½ oz) soya spread
4 tablespoons soya milk
3 tablespoons chopped
**   mixed herbs, such as**
**   tarragon, chives, parsley**
**   and fennel, plus extra**
**   leaves to garnish**
75 g (3 oz) smoked salmon,
**   cut into strips**
2 slices of grainy bread,
**   toasted**
salt and freshly ground black
**   pepper**

1 Put the tofu into a large bowl and break it up into small pieces using a fork. Add the eggs and a little salt and pepper and beat again.

2 Melt the soya spread in a small, heavy-based saucepan and add the milk and beaten egg mixture. Cook over a gentle heat, stirring with a wooden spoon, until lightly scrambled.

3 Stir the herbs and smoked salmon into the pan and season with plenty of pepper. Transfer the toast to warmed serving plates, spoon the scrambled eggs over it and garnish with a few herb leaves.

FAST FOOD TIP
Keep a pack of silken tofu in the store cupboard so that you can make this dish any time in minutes.

Smoked salmon Thai rolls

12 slices of smoked salmon
1 cucumber, peeled, deseeded and cut into matchsticks
1 long red chilli, deseeded and thinly sliced
handful each of fresh coriander, mint and Thai basil leaves

dressing
2 tablespoons sweet chilli sauce
2 tablespoons clear honey
2 tablespoons lime juice
1 tablespoon Thai fish sauce

1 Separate the smoked salmon slices and lay them flat on a work surface. Divide the cucumber, chilli and herbs between the smoked salmon slices, placing the ingredients in a mound on each slice.

2 Combine all the dressing ingredients in a bowl and drizzle over the filling. Roll up the salmon slices to enclose the filling and serve on a large platter.

FAST FOOD TIP
Thai basil leaves are usually available in Asian stores and have a wonderful aniseed flavour, but you can use ordinary sweet basil instead.

serves **4**
preparation time **5 minutes**
cooking time **10 minutes**

Sage and goats' cheese frittata

25 g (1 oz) butter, plus extra if
  necessary
18 large sage leaves
50 g (2 oz) soft goats' cheese,
  crumbled
2 tablespoons crème fraîche
4 eggs
salt and freshly ground black
  pepper
crusty bread, to serve

1 Melt the butter in a nonstick frying pan over a low heat and fry the sage leaves for 1–2 minutes until the leaves are crisp and golden and the butter is a lovely nutty brown colour. Remove 6 of the leaves and set aside. Pour the remaining leaves and butter into a bowl.

2 Beat the goats' cheese and crème fraîche together in a separate bowl until combined.

3 Beat the eggs in another bowl, season with salt and pepper, then stir in the sage butter. Reheat the frying pan (adding a little extra butter if necessary), then pour in the egg mixture and dot over spoonfuls of the goats' cheese mixture.

4 Cook over a medium heat for 4–5 minutes until the bottom is set, then transfer to a preheated hot grill to lightly brown the top.

5 Garnish with the reserved sage leaves and leave to cool slightly, then gently slip the frittata on to a plate and serve with crusty bread.

FAST FOOD TIP
A frittata is a flat Italian omelette, usually a combination of eggs, sautéed vegetables, herbs and sometimes topped with a little cheese.

---

serves **4**
preparation time **5 minutes**
cooking time **5 minutes**

Pan-fried haloumi
with lemon and paprika oil

**6 tablespoons extra virgin
  olive oil**
4 tablespoons lemon juice
½ teaspoon smoked paprika
**250 g (8 oz) haloumi cheese,
  cut into chunks**
**salt and freshly ground black
  pepper**

1 Combine the oil, lemon juice and paprika in a small bowl and season the mixture with salt and pepper.

2 Heat a heavy-based frying pan until hot, then add the haloumi and toss over a medium heat until golden and starting to soften.

3 Transfer immediately to a plate, drizzle over the flavoured oil and serve with cocktail sticks to spike the haloumi.

FAST FOOD TIP
Haloumi is a semi-hard ewes' milk cheese from Cyprus. It is often flavoured with chopped mint and has a wonderfully salty, sharp flavour and a delicious springy, chewy texture. It is perfectly suited to frying because it retains its shape – eat it as soon as it is cooked, while the outside is crisp and the inside is gooey and meltingly soft.

serves **4**
preparation time **10 minutes**
cooking time **8–10 minutes**

Fennel and marinated anchovy crostini

12 slices of French bread
1 fennel bulb, trimmed
1 small garlic clove, crushed
**2 tablespoons chopped flat
  leaf parsley**
**6 tablespoons extra virgin
  olive oil**
2 tablespoons lemon juice
**24 marinated anchovy fillets,
  drained**
**salt and freshly ground black
  pepper**

1 Arrange the bread slices on a baking sheet and bake in a preheated oven, 220ºC (425ºF), Gas Mark 7, for 8–10 minutes until crisp and golden, turning halfway through. Transfer to a platter.

2 Discard the tough outer layer of fennel leaves, cut the bulb in half lengthways and then cut crossways into wafer-thin slices – you will need about 100 g (3½ oz) of trimmed fennel. Put the fennel into a bowl with the garlic and parsley. Add the oil and lemon juice, season with salt and pepper and toss together until well coated.

3 Spoon the fennel mixture on to the crostini and top each with 2 anchovy fillets. Drizzle over any remaining dressing from the bowl, then serve.

FAST FOOD TIP
These wonderfully crisp, irresistible toasts can be served as part of an Italian antipasti selection.

serves **2–4**
preparation time **10 minutes**
cooking time **5 minutes**

Sun-blush bruschetta

2 tablespoons olive oil
½ small red onion, finely
   chopped
125 g (4 oz) firm tofu
50 g (2 oz) sun-blush
   tomatoes, chopped
3 tablespoons ready-made
   pesto
1 small garlic clove, crushed
4 chunky slices of country
   bread or ciabatta
small handful of basil leaves
salt and freshly ground black
   pepper

1 Heat 1 tablespoon of the oil in a small frying pan and fry the onion gently for 3 minutes until softened.

2 Pat the tofu dry on kitchen paper and crumble it into the pan. Add the tomatoes, pesto and a little salt and pepper to the pan and stir over a gentle heat for 2 minutes until hot.

3 Mix the remaining oil with the garlic. Toast the bread on both sides and brush with the garlic oil. Pile the tofu mixture on top and serve sprinkled with basil leaves.

FAST FOOD TIP
Even slightly stale bread can be put to good use in this simple starter. Any leftover topping will keep well in the refrigerator for a couple of days.

serves **4**
preparation time **10 minutes, plus marinating**
cooking time **about 7 minutes**

Grilled thyme-marinated goats' cheese

4 crottin de chèvre or small firm goats' cheese, halved horizontally
8 large vine leaves in brine, rinsed well in cold water
4 slices of walnut bread

marinade
225 ml (7½ fl oz) extra virgin olive oil, plus extra if necessary
50 ml (2 fl oz) walnut oil
1 teaspoon dried thyme or lemon thyme sprigs
grated rind of 1 lemon
1 teaspoon crushed dried red chillies
1 small garlic clove, thinly sliced
8 black peppercorns

to serve
green salad
balsamic vinegar

1 Put all the marinade ingredients into a 600 ml (1 pint) screw-top jar and mix well. Add the cheese halves and leave to marinate in a cool place for at least 24 hours and up to 3 days.

2 Remove the cheese from the marinade and drain on kitchen paper to remove any excess oil. Reserve the marinade. Place the vine leaves on a chopping board and put 1 cheese half in the centre of each. Wrap each leaf around the cheese so that it is completely sealed.

3 Toast the bread on both sides and keep it warm. Heat a ridged griddle pan over a medium heat. Put the parcels into the pan, seam side down, and cook for 4–5 minutes, turning once, until the leaves are crispy and the cheese is melting.

4 Serve the parcels immediately with the toasted bread and a little green salad, drizzled with the marinating oil and some balsamic vinegar.

Salads

Salads make perfect, healthful fast food, and here are some truly exciting combinations to spice up your mealtimes. Choose from peppered lamb, beetroot and watercress, gingered tofu and mango or Gorgonzola, spinach and walnuts.

serves **4**
preparation time **10 minutes**
cooking time **5–7 minutes**

Spiced chicken
and mango salad

4 boneless, skinless chicken
   breasts, about 150 g (5 oz)
   each
6 teaspoons mild curry paste
juice of 1 lemon
150 g (5 oz) natural bio yogurt
1 mango
50 g (2 oz) watercress
½ cucumber, diced
½ red onion, chopped
½ iceberg lettuce

FAST FOOD TIP
This healthy salad keeps the
fat content low by using a
natural yogurt dressing and
steaming the chicken.

1 Cut the chicken breasts into long, thin slices. Put
4 teaspoons of the curry paste into a plastic bag with the
lemon juice and mix by squeezing the bag. Add the chicken
and toss together.

2 Half-fill the base of a steamer with water and bring to the
boil. Put the chicken into the top of the steamer in a single
layer, cover and steam for 5 minutes until thoroughly
cooked. Test the chicken with a knife – the juices will run
clear when done.

3 Meanwhile, mix the remaining curry paste with the yogurt
in a bowl.

4 Cut a thick slice off either side of the mango to reveal the
large, flat stone, then make crisscross cuts in these slices
and scoop the flesh away from the skin using a spoon. Cut
away the flesh surrounding the stone and remove and
discard the skin.

5 Tear the watercress into bite-sized pieces. Add to the
yogurt dressing with the cucumber, onion and mango, and
toss together gently.

6 Tear the lettuce into pieces, divide it between 4 plates,
spoon the mango mixture on top and complete with the
warm chicken strips.

serves **4**
preparation time **15 minutes, plus resting**
cooking time **9–12 minutes**

Thai beef salad

**2 lean beef rump or sirloin
steaks, about 150 g (5 oz)
each, trimmed**
150 g (5 oz) baby sweetcorn
1 large cucumber
**1 small red onion, finely
chopped**
**3 tablespoons chopped fresh
coriander leaves**
4 tablespoons rice vinegar
**4 tablespoons sweet chilli
dipping sauce**
**2 tablespoons sesame seeds,
lightly toasted**

1 Heat a ridged griddle pan over a high heat. Put the steaks into the pan and cook for 3–4 minutes on each side. Leave to rest for 10–15 minutes, then thinly slice.

2 Meanwhile, put the sweetcorn into a saucepan of boiling water and cook for 3–4 minutes or until tender. Refresh under cold running water and drain well.

3 Slice the cucumber in half lengthways, then scoop out and discard the seeds using a small spoon. Cut the cucumber into 5 mm (¼ inch) slices.

4 Put the beef, sweetcorn, cucumber, onion and coriander into a large bowl. Stir in the vinegar and chilli sauce and mix well. Garnish the salad with sesame seeds and serve.

serves **4**
preparation time **10–15 minutes**
cooking time **5–6 minutes**

Smoked chicken
and avocado salad

6 tablespoons extra virgin olive oil
4 slices of day-old bread, cut into 1 cm (½ inch) dice
500 g (1 lb) smoked chicken breast slices
3 Little Gem or baby Cos lettuce hearts
1 large ripe avocado, peeled, stoned and diced
25 g (1 oz) freshly grated Parmesan cheese

dressing
125 ml (4 fl oz) extra virgin olive oil
2 tablespoons tarragon vinegar
1 tablespoon wholegrain mustard
1 tablespoon chopped tarragon
1 teaspoon caster sugar
salt and freshly ground black pepper

1 To make the croûtons, heat the oil in a frying pan and fry the bread cubes, stirring constantly, for 5–6 minutes until golden on all sides. Drain on kitchen paper.

2 Cut the chicken into bite-sized pieces and put into a large bowl. Separate the lettuce hearts into leaves and add to the bowl with the avocado, croûtons and Parmesan.

3 Whisk all the dressing ingredients together in a bowl and season with salt and pepper. Pour over the salad and toss well until it is evenly coated. Serve immediately.

FAST FOOD TIP
Because smoked chicken is hot-smoked, it is already cooked and ready to eat. If you are especially short of time, you can buy ready-made croûtons, but it is fairly simple to make your own.

serves **2**
preparation time **15 minutes, plus marinating**
cooking time **5 minutes**

Gingered tofu
and mango salad

125 g (4 oz) tofu
25 g (1 oz) fresh root ginger,
**   peeled and grated**
2 tablespoons light soy sauce
1 garlic clove, crushed
1 tablespoon seasoned rice
**   vinegar**
2 tablespoons groundnut or
**   soya oil**
1 bunch of spring onions,
**   trimmed and sliced**
**   diagonally into 1.5 cm**
**   (¾ inch) lengths**
40 g (1½ oz) cashew nuts
1 small mango, halved,
**   stoned, peeled and sliced**
½ small iceberg lettuce,
**   shredded**
2 tablespoons water

1 Pat the tofu dry on kitchen paper and cut into 1 cm
(½ inch) cubes. Put the ginger into a small bowl and mix in
the soy sauce, garlic and vinegar. Add the tofu to the bowl
and toss the ingredients together. Leave to marinate for
15 minutes.

2 Lift the tofu from the marinade with a fork, drain it and
reserve the marinade. Heat the oil in a frying pan and gently
fry the tofu for about 3 minutes until golden. Drain and keep
warm. Add the spring onions and cashews to the pan and fry
quickly for 30 seconds. Add the mango slices to the pan and
cook for 30 seconds until heated through.

3 Pile the lettuce on to serving plates and scatter the tofu,
spring onions, mango and cashews over the top. Heat the
marinade juices in the pan with the water, pour the mixture
over the salad and serve immediately.

FAST FOOD TIP
Tofu, also known as soya bean curd, is a soft, cheese-like
food made by curdling fresh hot soya milk with a coagulant.
It absorbs the flavours of any ingredients mixed with it.

serves **4**
preparation time **5 minutes**
cooking time **8 minutes**

Italian broccoli
and egg salad

4 eggs
300 g (10 oz) broccoli
2 small leeks, about 300 g
(10 oz), trimmed and
cleaned
wholemeal bread, to serve

tarragon and lemon dressing
juice of 1 lemon
2 tablespoons olive oil
2 teaspoons clear honey
1 tablespoon capers, well
drained
2 tablespoons chopped
tarragon, plus extra sprigs
to garnish (optional)
salt and freshly ground black
pepper

1 Half-fill the base of a steamer with water, add the eggs and bring to the boil. Cover with the steamer top and simmer for 8 minutes until hard-boiled.

2 Meanwhile, cut the broccoli into florets and thickly slice the broccoli stems and the leeks. Add the broccoli to the top of the steamer and cook for 3 minutes, then add the leeks and cook for a further 2 minutes.

3 To make the dressing, mix the lemon juice, oil, honey, capers and chopped tarragon together in a salad bowl and season with salt and pepper.

4 Crack the hard-boiled eggs, cool them quickly under cold running water, then remove and discard the shells and roughly chop the eggs.

5 Add the broccoli and leeks to the dressing, toss together and sprinkle with the chopped eggs. Garnish with extra tarragon sprigs, if you like, and serve warm with thickly sliced wholemeal bread.

serves **4**
preparation time **5 minutes**
cooking time **6–8 minutes**

Peppered lamb salad
with minted yogurt dressing

**2 teaspoons freshly ground
black pepper**
2 teaspoons salt
2 teaspoons ground cumin
**2 lamb loin fillets, about 250 g
(8 oz) each**
**extra virgin olive oil, for
brushing**
75 g (3 oz) watercress
**250 g (8 oz) vacuum-packed
cooked beetroot in natural
juices, drained and chopped**

mint yogurt
125 g (4 oz) Greek yogurt
1 tablespoon chopped mint
**salt and freshly ground black
pepper**

dressing
1 tablespoon walnut oil
**1 teaspoon white wine
vinegar**

1 Combine the pepper, salt and cumin on a plate, brush the lamb loins with olive oil and dip them into the pepper mixture to lightly coat the meat.

2 Heat a heavy-based frying pan over a high heat. Put the lamb loins into the pan and cook for 3–4 minutes on each side. Wrap them loosely in foil and leave to rest for 5 minutes

3 Meanwhile, combine the yogurt and mint in a bowl and season with salt and pepper. Whisk the walnut oil and vinegar for the dressing together in a small jug or cup.

4 Mix the watercress with the beetroot, drizzle with the dressing and arrange on serving plates.

5 Slice the lamb and serve with the salad and the minted yogurt.

> **FAST FOOD TIP**
> The meat used in this salad dish comes from the eye fillet, or tenderloin, which runs along the back of the lamb and is particularly sweet and tender.

Tomato, tofu
and hot pepper salad

**1 large beefsteak tomato,
   thinly sliced**
125 g (4 oz) firm tofu
**50 g (2 oz) hot piquante
   peppers, drained and
   thinly sliced**
3 tablespoons snipped chives
**2 tablespoons chopped flat
   leaf parsley**
50 g (2 oz) pine nuts, toasted
40 g (1½ oz) sultanas
4 tablespoons olive oil
2 tablespoons lemon juice
2 teaspoons caster sugar
**salt and freshly ground
   black pepper**
wholemeal bread, to serve

1 Arrange the tomato slices on 2 serving plates, lightly seasoning the layers with salt and pepper. Crumble the tofu into a bowl, then add the peppers, chives, parsley, pine nuts and sultanas and mix well.

2 Whisk the oil, lemon juice and sugar together in a jug or small bowl. Season lightly with salt and pepper and mix into the salad. Spoon the salad over the sliced tomatoes and serve with wholemeal bread for mopping up the juices.

FAST FOOD TIP
Use any canned or bottled peppers to add plenty of sweetness and bite to this salad, but make sure they're not too fiery.

serves **4**
preparation time **15 minutes**

Orange and avocado salad

4 large juicy oranges
2 small ripe avocados, peeled
  and stoned
2 teaspoons cardamom pods
3 tablespoons light olive oil
1 tablespoon clear honey
pinch of ground allspice
2 teaspoons lemon juice
salt and freshly ground
  black pepper
watercress sprigs, to garnish

1 Peel the oranges and remove the white pith. Working over a bowl to catch the juice, cut between each membrane to remove the segments. Slice the avocados and toss gently with the orange segments. Pile on to serving plates.

2 Reserve a few whole cardamom pods for garnishing. Crush the remainder using a mortar and pestle to extract the seeds, or put into a small bowl and crush with the end of a rolling pin. Pick out and discard the pods.

3 Mix the cardamom seeds with the oil, honey, allspice and lemon juice in a bowl and season with salt and pepper, then stir in the reserved orange juice.

4 Garnish the salads with the watercress sprigs and reserved cardamom pods, spoon the dressing over the top and serve.

serves **4**
preparation time **5 minutes**

Fig, mozzarella
and prosciutto salad

8–12 ripe black figs
250 g (8 oz) buffalo
    mozzarella cheese
8 slices of prosciutto
a few basil leaves

dressing
3 tablespoons extra virgin
    olive oil
1 tablespoon verjuice
salt and freshly ground
    black pepper

1 Cut the figs into quarters, tear the mozzarella and prosciutto into bite-sized pieces and arrange on a large platter with the basil leaves.

2 Whisk the dressing ingredients together in a jug or small bowl and season with salt and pepper. Drizzle over the salad and serve immediately.

FAST FOOD TIP
Verjuice, made from unripe grapes, has a strong, acidic flavour and is used in cooking as an alternative to lemon juice or vinegar. It gives the dressing a lovely flavour, but if you cannot find it, use good-quality white wine vinegar sweetened with a pinch of sugar instead.

serves **4**
preparation time **15 minutes**
cooking time **about 5 minutes**

Asparagus salad
with tarragon and lemon dressing

**3 tablespoons olive oil
(optional)**
**500 g (1 lb) asparagus,
trimmed**
**100 ml (3½ fl oz) Tarragon and
Lemon Dressing
(see page 37)**
**125 g (4 oz) rocket or other
salad leaves**
**2 spring onions, trimmed
and finely sliced**
4 radishes, finely sliced
**salt and freshly ground black
pepper**

to garnish
**roughly chopped mixed herbs,
such as tarragon, parsley,
chervil and dill**
thin strips of lemon rind

1 Heat the oil, if using, in a frying pan and add the asparagus in a single layer. Cook for about 5 minutes, turning occasionally. The asparagus should be tender when pierced with the tip of a sharp knife, and lightly patched with brown. Transfer from the pan to a shallow dish and sprinkle with salt and pepper. Pour over the Tarragon and Lemon Dressing and toss gently, then leave to stand for 5 minutes.

2 Arrange the rocket or other salad leaves on a platter, sprinkle the spring onions and radishes over the top and arrange the asparagus in a pile in the middle of the leaves. Garnish with chopped herbs and the lemon rind. Serve on its own with bread or as an accompaniment to a main dish.

FAST FOOD TIP
This simple dish can be made in the morning and left to marinate all day, to serve at supper. Trim the ends of the asparagus stalks by cutting them across at a sharp angle just where the bright green colour starts to fade into a dull green.

serves **4**
preparation **10 minutes, plus standing**
cooking time **5 minutes**

Spiced couscous salad

200 ml (7 fl oz) vegetable stock
200 ml (7 fl oz) orange juice
1 teaspoon ground cinnamon
½ teaspoon ground coriander
250 g (8 oz) instant couscous
75 g (3 oz) raisins
2 ripe tomatoes, chopped
¼ preserved lemon, chopped (optional)
½ bunch of flat leaf parsley, roughly chopped
½ bunch of mint, roughly chopped
1 garlic clove, crushed
4 tablespoons extra virgin olive oil
salt and freshly ground black pepper

1 Combine the stock, orange juice, spices and ½ teaspoon of salt in a saucepan. Bring to the boil, then stir in the couscous and remove the pan from the heat. Cover and leave to stand for 10 minutes.

2 Combine the raisins, tomatoes, preserved lemon, if using, herbs, garlic and oil in a large bowl, stir in the soaked couscous and season with salt and pepper. Serve warm or leave to cool and serve at room temperature.

FAST FOOD TIP
Choose instant couscous for this recipe because it needs only to be soaked in boiling water; some types can need longer cooking times.

serves **4**
preparation time **10 minutes**
cooking time **3 minutes**

Salad of spinach,
Gorgonzola and honeyed walnuts

1 tablespoon clear honey
125 g (4 oz) walnut halves
250 g (8 oz) French beans, trimmed
200 g (7 oz) baby spinach leaves
150 g (5 oz) Gorgonzola cheese, crumbled

dressing
4 tablespoons walnut oil
2 tablespoons extra virgin olive oil
1–2 tablespoons sherry vinegar
salt and freshly ground black pepper

1 Heat the honey in a small frying pan over a medium heat and stir-fry the walnuts for 2–3 minutes until the nuts are glazed. Tip them on to a plate and leave to cool.

2 Meanwhile, bring a saucepan of lightly salted water to the boil, add the beans and cook for 3 minutes. Drain, refresh under cold running water and shake dry. Put into a large bowl with the spinach leaves.

3 Whisk the dressing ingredients together in a jug or small bowl and season with salt and pepper. Pour over the salad and toss well to coat the leaves and beans. Arrange the salad in bowls, scatter over the Gorgonzola and honeyed walnuts and serve immediately.

FAST FOOD TIP
Gorgonzola has a strong, piquant taste and wonderfully creamy texture. If you prefer a milder flavour, use a less-robust blue cheese such as dolcelatte instead.

Meat

These recipes prove that speed and sophistication can go together. Glazed lamb noisettes and chillied hamburgers come seared and succulent from the griddle, while tender pork medallions and lambs' liver with their fruity sauces are one-pan prepared.

serves **4**
preparation time **5 minutes**
cooking time **12–15 minutes**

Pork medallions
with sherried figs

2 tablespoons olive oil
8 pork medallions, about 675 g
(1 lb 6 oz) in total
2 onions, thinly sliced
2 garlic cloves, crushed
150 g (5 oz) ready-to-eat dried
figs, thickly sliced
125 ml (4 fl oz) cream sherry
or Marsala
300 ml (½ pint) chicken stock
3 teaspoons thick honey
2 tablespoons crème fraîche
salt and freshly ground black
pepper
buttered soft polenta,
to serve

to garnish
torn flat leaf parsley leaves
paprika

1 Heat the oil in a large frying pan over a high heat and fry the pork until browned on one side. Turn the pork over and add the onions and garlic. Fry for a further 5 minutes, turning the pork once or twice and stirring the onions, until both are browned.

2 Add the figs with the sherry or Marsala, stock and honey and season with salt and pepper. Cook over a medium heat for 5 minutes until the sauce has reduced and the pork is thoroughly cooked.

3 Stir in the crème fraîche, then garnish with the parsley and a little paprika and serve on a bed of polenta.

FAST FOOD TIP
Look out for extra-trimmed, lean pork loin steaks, or medallions, in the supermarket – they are ideal for this deliciously easy Italian-style dish.

serves **4**
preparation time **5 minutes**
cooking time **10 minutes**

Seared lamb noisettes
with leek and caper confetti

8 lamb loin chops
3 tablespoons redcurrant
jelly
1 tablespoon olive oil
25 g (1 oz) butter
2 leeks, trimmed, cleaned
and thinly sliced
1 tablespoon capers, drained
and rinsed
small handful of rosemary or
mint leaves, snipped, plus
extra to garnish
2 teaspoons pink
peppercorns in brine,
drained
salt and freshly ground black
pepper

1 Roll up the lamb chops tightly and secure each with 2 cocktail sticks. Put the chops into a foil-lined grill pan, dot with the redcurrant jelly and season with salt and pepper. Cook under a preheated hot grill for 5 minutes, then turn them over, spoon the redcurrant jelly juices over the lamb and cook for a further 5 minutes.

2 Meanwhile, heat the oil and butter in a frying pan and stir-fry the leeks, capers, snipped herbs and peppercorns for 5 minutes until softened and just beginning to brown. Spoon on to individual plates.

3 Arrange the lamb on top of the leek mixture, remove the cocktail sticks and sprinkle with extra snipped herbs.

serves **4**
preparation time **10 minutes, plus marinating (optional)**
cooking time **30 minutes**

Roasted chilli pork parcels

400 g (13 oz) pork fillet
3 tablespoons dark soy sauce
2 tablespoons chilli sauce
¼ teaspoon Chinese
  five-spice powder
1 teaspoon clear honey

to serve
1 Little Gem lettuce, leaves
  separated
500 g (1 lb) cooked
  basmati rice
large handful of mint leaves
100 g (3½ oz) baby cherry
  tomatoes, quartered

1 Rub the pork with the soy sauce, chilli sauce, five-spice powder and honey. Cover and leave to marinate in the refrigerator if time allows.

2 Line a roasting tray with foil and place the pork on top. Cover with more foil and cook in a preheated oven, 190°C (375°F), Gas Mark 5, for 20 minutes. Remove the foil and roast for a further 10 minutes or until cooked through. Leave to rest for 5 minutes and then slice.

3 Put all the accompaniments into separate bowls and allow everyone to assemble their own rolls. Take a lettuce leaf and fill it with a spoonful of rice, a few mint leaves, tomato quarters and pork slices. Roll up the lettuce leaf and eat with your hands.

FAST FOOD TIP
The Vietnamese often use lettuce leaves as a wrapper for spicy fillings. If you want to try something a bit different, why not add some cooked bean thread noodles or even some freshly sliced mango to these delicate lettuce-leaf parcels.

serves **4**
preparation time **5 minutes**
cooking time **15 minutes**

Lambs' liver with cranberries and bacon

2 tablespoons olive oil
2 onions, thinly sliced
150 g (5 oz) smoked back
   bacon, diced
25 g (1 oz) butter
625 g (1¼ lb) sliced lambs'
   liver
2 tablespoons cranberry
   sauce
2 tablespoons red wine
   vinegar
75 g (3 oz) frozen cranberries
2 tablespoons water
salt and freshly ground black
   pepper
mashed potatoes, to serve

1 Heat the oil in a large frying pan over a medium heat and fry the onions and bacon for 10 minutes, stirring occasionally, until they are a deep golden brown. Remove from the pan and set aside.

2 Melt the butter in the pan over a high heat and fry the liver for 3 minutes, turning once or twice, until browned on the outside and just pink in the centre.

3 Add the cranberry sauce, vinegar, cranberries and water to the pan. Season with salt and pepper and cook for 2 minutes, stirring, until the cranberry sauce has melted and the cranberries are soft and heated through.

4 Stir in the fried onions and bacon, then serve with mashed potatoes.

FAST FOOD TIP
Lambs' liver has a wonderful flavour and succulent texture. It takes only the briefest time to cook, so be careful not to overcook it.

serves **4**
preparation time **10 minutes**
cooking time **6–14 minutes**

Red-hot hamburgers

575 g (1 lb 3 oz) minced beef
2 garlic cloves, crushed
1 red onion, finely chopped
1 red chilli, finely chopped
1 bunch of flat leaf parsley,
 chopped
1 tablespoon Worcestershire
 sauce
1 egg, beaten
4 wholegrain hamburger
 buns, split
spicy salad leaves, such
 as rocket or mizuna
1 beefsteak tomato, sliced
salt and freshly ground
 black pepper
relish or tomato sauce, to
 serve (optional)

1 Put the minced beef into a large bowl, add the garlic, onion, chilli, parsley, Worcestershire sauce, beaten egg and a little salt and pepper and mix well.

2 Heat a ridged griddle pan over a high heat. Divide the beef mixture into 4 pieces and shape into burgers. Put the burgers into the pan and cook for 3 minutes on each side for rare, 5 minutes for medium or 7 minutes for well done.

3 Grill the bun halves quickly under a preheated hot grill. Fill each bun with some salad leaves, tomato slices and a grilled burger. Serve with relish or tomato sauce, if you like.

FAST FOOD TIP
These burgers can also be made with minced lamb and served in pitta bread, if preferred.

serves **4**
preparation time **5 minutes**
cooking time **15 minutes**

Oven-roasted pork fillet
with almond and parsley pesto

2 pork tenderloin fillets,
about 400 g (13 oz) each
6 tablespoons extra virgin
olive oil
50 g (2 oz) blanched almonds
1 garlic clove, crushed
1 bunch of flat leaf parsley
2 tablespoons freshly grated
Parmesan cheese
salt and freshly ground
black pepper

to serve
boiled new potatoes
green salad

1 Trim off any gristle from the pork fillets, cut them in half crossways and season with salt and pepper. Heat 1 tablespoon of the oil in a frying pan and fry the meat for 2–3 minutes until browned on all sides. Transfer to a roasting dish and cook in a preheated oven, 190°C (375°F), Gas Mark 5, for 15 minutes until cooked through. Remove from the oven, wrap in foil and leave to rest for 5 minutes.

2 Meanwhile, dry-fry the almonds in a clean frying pan, stirring until browned, then leave to cool slightly. Put into a food processor with the garlic, parsley, remaining oil and salt and pepper and whiz to a fairly smooth paste. Alternatively, pound the ingredients together using a pestle and mortar. Stir in the Parmesan and adjust the seasoning if necessary.

3 Slice the pork, arrange it on serving plates with any pan juices and serve with boiled new potatoes and a green salad, drizzled with spoonfuls of the almond and parsley pesto.

FAST FOOD TIP
Pork fillet is a particularly lean cut of meat, making it a healthy option. However, you could use pork chops instead of fillet.

serves **4**
preparation time **5 minutes**
cooking time **6–7 minutes**

Pizza bianchi

4 x 20 cm (8 inch)
  Mediterranean flatbreads
200 g (7 oz) Gorgonzola or
  dolcelatte cheese,
  crumbled
8 slices of prosciutto
50 g (2 oz) wild rocket
freshly ground black pepper
extra virgin olive oil, for
  drizzling

1 Put the flatbreads on to 2 baking sheets and scatter the centres with the cheese. Bake in a preheated oven, 200°C (400°F), Gas Mark 6, for 6–7 minutes until the cheese has melted and the bases are crisp.

2 Top each pizza with 2 slices of prosciutto and some rocket, then grind over some pepper and drizzle with oil. Serve immediately.

Poultry

Poultry is both highly versatile and quick to cook – here is a host of inspiring ideas for meals in minutes. Choose from aromatic skewers and wraps, tasty chargrilled breasts and spicy stir-fries, along with a super-simple oven-baked risotto.

serves **4**
preparation time **5 minutes**
cooking time **25 minutes**

Chicken, pea
and mint risotto

25 g (1 oz) butter
1 onion, finely chopped
150 g (5 oz) boneless, skinless
  chicken breast, cut
  into strips
200 g (7 oz) arborio or
  risotto rice
1 teaspoon fennel seeds
900 ml (1½ pints) hot chicken
  stock
75 g (3 oz) frozen peas,
  thawed
juice and grated rind
  of 1 lemon
2 tablespoons double cream
100 g (3½ oz) Parmesan
  cheese, grated
2 tablespoons chopped mint
salt and freshly ground
  black pepper

1 Melt the butter in a heatproof casserole and fry the onion and chicken for 3 minutes. Add the rice and fennel seeds and stir-fry for 30 seconds, then add the stock and peas.

2 Cover tightly and cook in a preheated oven, 200°C (400°F), Gas Mark 6, for 20 minutes until the rice is tender and all the liquid has been absorbed.

3 Remove from the oven, stir in the lemon juice and rind, cream and Parmesan and season with salt and pepper. Re-cover the casserole and leave to stand for 2 minutes, then stir in the mint. Serve immediately.

FAST FOOD TIP
Risotto cooked in the oven is incredibly simple. The result is not usually as creamy as a risotto stirred on the hob, but this recipe includes a little cream to add at the end to make up for it. Be sure to use arborio or another risotto rice because you cannot achieve the taste and texture of an authentic risotto using any other rice variety.

serves **4**
preparation time **10 minutes**
cooking time **about 8 minutes**

Thai chicken
with basil, chilli and cashews

2 tablespoons vegetable oil
750 g (1½ lb) boneless,
  skinless chicken breasts,
  thinly sliced
4 garlic cloves, crushed
2 large green chillies,
  deseeded and chopped
1 onion, cut into chunks
1 green pepper, cored,
  deseeded and cut into
  chunks
5 tablespoons Thai fish sauce
2 tablespoons dark soy sauce
2 tablespoons soft brown
  sugar

to serve
large handful of cashew nuts
15 g (½ oz) Thai basil or fresh
  coriander leaves
plain boiled rice, to serve

1 Heat the oil in a wok over a high heat until smoking and stir-fry the chicken, garlic and chillies for 1 minute, then add the onion and green pepper. Continue stir-frying for 5 minutes until the chicken is cooked through.

2 Add the fish sauce, soy sauce and sugar and mix well. Bring to the boil, then transfer to a serving dish. Scatter with the cashews and basil or coriander and serve with boiled rice.

serves **4**
preparation time **15 minutes, plus chilling**
cooking time **10 minutes**

Chicken fajitas

1 tablespoon olive oil
1 large red onion, thinly sliced
1 red pepper, cored, deseeded
 and thinly sliced
1 yellow pepper, cored,
 deseeded and thinly sliced
450 g (14½ oz) boneless,
 skinless chicken breasts,
 sliced into thin strips
⅛ teaspoon paprika
⅛ teaspoon mild chilli powder
⅛ teaspoon ground cumin
¼ teaspoon dried oregano
4 soft flour tortillas
½ iceberg lettuce, finely
 shredded
guacamole, to serve (optional)

tomato salsa
1 small red onion, finely
 chopped
425 g (14 oz) small vine-
 ripened tomatoes
2 garlic cloves, crushed
large handful of fresh
 coriander leaves, chopped
freshly ground black pepper

1 First prepare the tomato salsa. Combine the chopped onion, tomatoes, garlic and coriander in a bowl. Season with pepper, then cover and chill for 30 minutes to allow the flavours to develop.

2 Heat the oil in a wok or large nonstick frying pan. Add the sliced onion and peppers for 3–4 minutes. Add the chicken, paprika, chilli powder, cumin and oregano and stir-fry for 5 minutes until the chicken is cooked through.

3 Meanwhile, wrap the tortillas in foil and warm in the oven for 5 minutes or according to the packet instructions.

4 Spoon one-quarter of the chicken mixture into the centre of each tortilla, then add a couple of tablespoons of the salsa and some shredded lettuce. Roll up and serve warm, accompanied by guacamole, if you like.

serves **4**
preparation time **10 minutes**
cooking time **8–10 minutes**

Chicken teriyaki

**750 g (1½ lb) boneless,
  skinless chicken breasts,
  cubed**
**12 spring onions, trimmed
  and cut into 5 cm (2 inch)
  lengths**
**2 red peppers, cored,
  deseeded and cut into
  chunks**
2 tablespoons vegetable oil
plain boiled rice, to serve

teriyaki sauce
3 tablespoons dark soy sauce
3 tablespoons clear honey
**3 tablespoons sake or
  dry sherry**
1 garlic clove, crushed
**3 slices of peeled fresh
  root ginger**

1 Put all the sauce ingredients into a small saucepan and simmer for 5 minutes until thickened.

2 Meanwhile, divide the chicken, spring onions and red peppers between 8 pre-soaked bamboo skewers and brush with the oil.

3 Cook the chicken skewers in a preheated ridged griddle pan or under a preheated hot grill for 4 minutes on each side or until cooked through. Brush with the teriyaki sauce and serve on a bed of boiled rice, drizzled with more sauce.

FAST FOOD TIP
Sake is widely used in Japanese cooking and adds an authentic flavour. However, if you don't have any to hand, you can use dry sherry instead. Try to use Japanese-brewed soy sauce, rather than Chinese soy sauce, which has a much saltier, less malty taste.

serves **4**
preparation time **5 minutes**
cooking time **8 minutes**

Warm turkey focaccia

1 tablespoon olive oil
250 g (8 oz) boneless, skinless turkey fillet, cut into thin strips
1 onion, thinly sliced
2 focaccia loaves, thickly sliced
2 tablespoons black olive tapenade
100 g (3½ oz) sun-dried tomatoes in oil, drained and sliced
4 tomatoes, roughly chopped
handful of basil leaves (optional)
salt and freshly ground black pepper
rocket leaves, to garnish

1 Heat the oil in a large frying pan over a high heat and stir-fry the turkey and onion for 5 minutes until browned.

2 Meanwhile, lightly toast the focaccia slices on both sides. Spread thinly with the tapenade and drizzle with a little oil from the jar of sun-dried tomatoes.

3 Add the fresh and sun-dried tomatoes to the turkey with the basil leaves, if using, and season with salt and pepper. Cook for 3 minutes, then spoon on to the toasted focaccia and garnish with rocket leaves. Serve immediately.

serves **4**
preparation time **10 minutes**
cooking time **7 minutes**

Aromatic chicken pancakes

**4 boneless, skinless chicken
  breasts, about 150 g
  (5 oz) each**
6 tablespoons hoisin sauce

to serve
12 Chinese pancakes
**½ cucumber, cut into
  matchsticks**
**12 spring onions, trimmed
  and thinly sliced**
**handful of fresh coriander
  leaves**
**4 tablespoons hoisin sauce
  mixed with 3 tablespoons
  water**

1 Place the chicken breasts between 2 sheets of clingfilm or nonstick baking paper and flatten them with a rolling pin until they are 2.5 cm (1 inch) thick. Remove from the clingfilm or paper, lay them on a baking sheet and brush with the hoisin sauce.

2 Cook the chicken breasts under a preheated hot grill for 4 minutes. Turn them over, brush with more hoisin sauce and grill for a further 3 minutes or until the chicken is cooked through.

3 Meanwhile, warm the pancakes in a bamboo steamer for 3 minutes or until heated through.

4 Thinly slice the chicken and arrange on a serving plate. Put the cucumber, spring onions and coriander into a bowl and the diluted hoisin sauce in a separate dish. Serve with the warm pancakes and allow everyone to assemble their own filled pancakes.

serves **4**
preparation time **5 minutes**
cooking time **10 minutes**

Nasi goreng

2 tablespoons vegetable oil
150 g (5 oz) boneless, skinless
chicken breast, finely
chopped
50 g (2 oz) cooked peeled
prawns
1 garlic clove, crushed
1 carrot, grated
¼ white cabbage,
thinly sliced
1 egg, beaten
300 g (10 oz) cold cooked
basmati rice
2 tablespoons ketchup manis
(sweet soy sauce)
½ teaspoon sesame oil
1 tablespoon chilli sauce
1 red chilli, deseeded and
sliced into strips

1 Heat the vegetable oil in a wok over a high heat until smoking and stir-fry the chicken for 1 minute. Add the prawns, garlic, carrot and cabbage and stir-fry for a further 3–4 minutes.

2 Pour in the egg and spread it out using a wooden spoon. Let it set, then add the rice and break up the egg, stirring it in.

3 Add the ketchup manis, sesame oil and chilli sauce and heat through, then serve, garnished with the strips of chilli.

serves **2**
preparation time **10 minutes**
cooking time **about 20 minutes**

Duck with cinnamon
and redcurrant sauce

**2 boneless duck breasts,
    about 300 g (10 oz) each**
1 tablespoon olive oil
**1 small red onion, finely
    chopped**
1 garlic clove, finely chopped
200 ml (7 fl oz) chicken stock
200 ml (7 fl oz) red wine
pinch of ground cinnamon
**1 tablespoon reduced-sugar
    redcurrant jelly**
freshly ground black pepper

to serve (optional)
Puy lentils
sugar snap peas

1 Heat a heavy-based frying pan or ridged griddle pan over a high heat. Put the duck breasts, skin side down, into the pan and cook for 2–3 minutes or until brown. Turn them over and brown the other side. (By browning them skin side down first, there should be no need to add any fat.)

2 Transfer the duck breasts to a roasting tin and cook in a preheated oven, 200°C (400°F), Gas Mark 6, for 15 minutes or until cooked through.

3 Meanwhile, heat the oil in a nonstick frying pan and fry the onion and garlic for 2–3 minutes. Add the stock, wine and cinnamon and bring to the boil. Allow to bubble for 10 minutes or until reduced by half. Strain the sauce and discard the onion. Season with pepper and stir in the redcurrant jelly.

4 Thickly slice the duck and transfer to 2 warmed plates. Spoon over a little of the sauce and serve with Puy lentils and sugar snap peas, if you like.

serves **4**
preparation time **10 minutes**
cooking time **18–20 minutes**

Blue cheese
and chicken wraps

4 boneless, skinless chicken
    breasts, about 150 g
    (5 oz) each
125 g (4 oz) Gorgonzola
    cheese, cut into 4 pieces
4 sun-dried tomatoes in oil,
    drained
4 slices of Serrano ham,
    about 50 g (2 oz) in total
2 tablespoons olive oil
salt and freshly ground
    black pepper

to serve
griddled asparagus
griddled tomatoes
    on the vine

1 Cut a slit through the side of each chicken breast and enlarge it to make a small pocket. Tuck a piece of Gorgonzola and a sun-dried tomato into each pocket, season with salt and pepper, then wrap each breast in a slice of ham.

2 Put the chicken breasts, the join in the ham downwards, on to a foil-lined baking sheet and drizzle with the oil. Cook in a preheated oven, 190ºC (375ºF), Gas Mark 5, for 18–20 minutes until the ham has darkened and the chicken is cooked through.

3 Transfer to individual plates and serve with griddled asparagus and tomatoes on the vine.

FAST FOOD TIP
The chicken wraps can be prepared ahead of time and popped in the oven just before you're ready to eat. For a slightly milder-tasting dish, use brie, Camembert or Cheddar instead of Gorgonzola cheese.

serves **4**
preparation time **5 minutes, plus marinating**
cooking time **16 minutes**

Chargrilled chicken
with coriander salsa

2 tablespoons dark soy sauce
2 teaspoons sesame oil
1 tablespoon olive oil
2 teaspoons clear honey
pinch of dried red chilli flakes
4 large boneless, skinless
   chicken breasts, about
   200 g (7 oz) each

coriander salsa
1 red onion, diced
1 small garlic clove, crushed
1 bunch of fresh coriander,
   roughly chopped
6 tablespoons extra virgin
   olive oil
grated rind and juice of
   1 lemon
1 teaspoon ground cumin
salt and freshly ground
   black pepper

to serve
steamed couscous
diced tomato

1 Combine the soy sauce, sesame oil, olive oil, honey and chilli flakes in a shallow dish, add the chicken, cover and leave to marinate in the refrigerator for as long as possible.

2 Lift the chicken out of the marinade and reserve the marinade. Heat a ridged griddle pan over a high heat. Put the chicken breasts into the pan and cook over a medium heat for 8 minutes on each side until charred and cooked through. Wrap in foil and leave to rest for 5 minutes.

3 Meanwhile, mix all the salsa ingredients together in a bowl and season with salt and pepper. Set aside to allow the flavours to infuse. Strain the marinade juices into a small saucepan and bring to the boil, then remove from the heat and keep warm.

4 Serve the chicken with the couscous tossed with diced tomato and top with the salsa and the marinade sauce.

> **FAST FOOD TIP**
> To ensure the chicken is nicely chargrilled on the outside and moist and tender on the inside, preheat the griddle pan until hot, then reduce the heat to medium as you add the chicken.

Fish and Seafood

Fish and seafood are ultra-fast to cook and mostly come pre-prepared. Here, their natural flavours are given imaginative treatments – squid with a lime and coconut dressing, scallops with a soy and ginger glaze and salmon with a five-spice coating.

serves **4**
preparation time **10 minutes, plus marinating**
cooking time **5 minutes**

Mediterranean swordfish skewers
with peppers and mango

500 g (1 lb) skinned swordfish steak, cut into large cubes
1 green pepper, cored, deseeded and cut into 2.5 cm (1 inch) pieces
1 red pepper, cored, deseeded and cut into 2.5 cm (1 inch) pieces
1 red onion, cut into quarters
1 ripe but firm mango, halved, stoned, peeled and cut into thick slices

marinade
2–3 thyme sprigs
leaves from 1–2 rosemary sprigs
grated rind of 1 lemon
1 garlic clove, lightly crushed
100 ml (3½ fl oz) olive oil
2 teaspoons fennel seeds
freshly ground black pepper

1 Mix all the marinade ingredients together in a bowl and put into a large, shallow dish with the swordfish cubes, peppers, onion and mango. Cover and set aside at room temperature for about 1 hour.

2 Heat a ridged griddle pan over a medium heat. Thread the swordfish, peppers, onion and mango on to skewers. If you are using rosemary sprigs (see below), cover any leaves that are still attached to the ends with a piece of foil to prevent them from burning. Put the skewers into the pan and cook for about 5 minutes until the fish is cooked through, turning occasionally. Serve immediately.

FAST FOOD TIP
Rather than using metal skewers, use bamboo skewers soaked in warm water for about 20 minutes, or try sharpened rosemary sprigs with the leaves removed for extra flavour.

serves **4**
preparation time **10 minutes**
cooking time **15 minutes**

Mackerel
with lemons and olives

**4 mackerel, about 300 g
 (10 oz) each, gutted
 and heads removed
1 small bunch of thyme,
 bruised
1 teaspoon cumin seeds,
 bruised
2 tablespoons extra virgin
 olive oil, plus extra for
 drizzling
1 lemon, sliced
2 bay leaves
125 g (4 oz) black olives
2 tablespoons lemon juice
salt and freshly ground
 black pepper
tomato, basil and onion
 salad, to serve**

1 Use a sharp knife to make 3 slashes in each side of each fish. Combine the thyme, cumin and oil, season with salt and pepper and rub all over the fish, making sure some of the flavourings are pressed into the cuts.

2 Arrange the mackerel in a roasting tin and scatter over the lemon slices, bay leaves and olives. Drizzle with the lemon juice and a little extra oil, season with salt and pepper and cook in a preheated oven, 220°C (425°F), Gas Mark 7, for 15 minutes until the fish are cooked through. Serve with a tomato, basil and onion salad.

FAST FOOD TIP
Bruising the thyme and cumin seeds helps to release their flavour. The easiest way to do this is in a pestle and mortar, or on a chopping board with a rolling pin.

serves **4**
preparation time **10–15 minutes**
cooking time **12–14 minutes**

Stuffed monkfish
with balsamic dressing

**100 ml (3½ fl oz) balsamic
vinegar**
**4 monkfish fillets, about 150 g
(5 oz) each**
**4 teaspoons good-quality
tapenade**
8 basil leaves
**8 rashers of bacon, derinded
and stretched with the back
of a knife**
375 g (12 oz) green beans
150 g (5 oz) frozen peas
**6 spring onions, trimmed
and finely sliced**
**125 g (4 oz) feta cheese,
crumbled**
2 tablespoons basil oil
salt

1 Pour the vinegar into a small saucepan. Bring to the boil over a medium heat, then reduce the heat and simmer for 8–10 minutes until thick and glossy. Set aside to cool slightly, but keep warm.

2 Place the monkfish on a chopping board and, using a sharp knife, make a deep incision about 5 cm (2 inches) long in the side of each fillet. Stuff each with 1 teaspoon of the tapenade and 2 basil leaves. Wrap 2 bacon rashers around each fillet, sealing in the filling. Fasten with a cocktail stick.

3 Bring a saucepan of salted water to the boil, add the beans and cook for 3 minutes. Add the peas and cook for a further minute, then drain and keep warm.

4 Heat a ridged griddle pan over a medium heat. Put the monkfish fillets into the pan and cook for 4–5 minutes on each side or until the fish is cooked through. Remove from the heat and leave to rest for a minute or two.

5 Meanwhile, toss the beans and peas with the spring onions, feta and basil oil and arrange on 4 serving plates. Top each with a monkfish fillet and serve immediately, drizzled with the warm balsamic dressing.

serves **4**
preparation time **10 minutes, plus cooling and marinating**
cooking time **15–20 minutes**

Grilled miso cod
with pak choi

**4 chunky cod fillets, about
175 g (6 oz) each
olive oil, for brushing
4 heads of pak choi, halved
lengthways and blanched
in boiling water for
1–2 minutes**

miso sauce
**100 g (3½ oz) miso paste
50 ml (2 fl oz) soy sauce
50 ml (2 fl oz) sake
50 ml (2 fl oz) rice wine (mirin)
50 g (2 oz) caster sugar**

1 First prepare the miso sauce. Put all the sauce ingredients into a small saucepan and heat gently until the sugar has dissolved. Simmer very gently for about 5 minutes, stirring frequently. Remove from the heat and leave to cool.

2 Arrange the cod fillets in a snug-fitting dish and cover with the cold miso sauce. Rub the sauce over the fillets so that they are completely covered, cover the dish and leave to marinate in the refrigerator for at least 6 hours, but preferably overnight.

3 Heat a ridged griddle pan over a medium heat. Remove the cod fillets from the miso sauce, put into the pan and cook for 2–3 minutes, then carefully turn them over and cook for a further 2–3 minutes. Remove and keep warm.

4 Clean the griddle pan and reheat. Brush a little oil over the cut side of the pak choi, then place it, cut side down, in the pan and cook for 2 minutes or until hot and lightly charred. Arrange on a serving plate with the cod. Serve immediately.

> **FAST FOOD TIP**
> Miso is a fermented soya bean paste from Japan, which can be used to marinate any type of firm white fish.

serves **4**
preparation time **5 minutes**
cooking time **6 minutes**

Grilled lemon sole
with caper and herb sauce

**4 lemon sole, about 300 g
   (10 oz) each, skinned**
**1 tablespoon extra virgin
   olive oil**
150 g (5 oz) butter
**8 tablespoons baby capers,
   drained**
**2 tablespoons chopped flat
   leaf parsley**
2 tablespoons snipped chives
4 tablespoons lemon juice
**salt and freshly ground
   black pepper**

to serve
steamed carrot batons
steamed courgette batons

1 Brush the lemon sole with the oil and season with salt and pepper on both sides. Put into a foil-lined grill pan and cook under a preheated hot grill for 3 minutes on each side. Transfer to warmed serving plates, cover with foil and leave to rest for 5 minutes.

2 Meanwhile, melt the butter in a saucepan and gently fry the capers for 1 minute. Add the herbs and lemon juice, season with pepper and remove from the heat. Pour the sauce over the sole and serve immediately with steamed carrot and courgette batons.

FAST FOOD TIP
Lemon sole are large fish, so unless you have a large grill pan, cook the fish two at a time.

serves **4**
preparation time **10 minutes**
cooking time **15 minutes**

Roasted cod
with prosciutto, cherry tomatoes and olives

375 g (12 oz) cherry tomatoes, halved
50 g (2 oz) pitted black olives
2 tablespoons capers, drained and rinsed
grated rind and juice of 1 lemon
2 teaspoons chopped thyme
4 tablespoons extra virgin olive oil
4 cod fillets, about 175 g (6 oz) each
4 slices of prosciutto
salt and freshly ground black pepper

to serve (optional)
new potatoes
green salad

1 Combine the tomatoes, olives, capers, lemon rind, thyme and oil in a roasting tin and season with salt and pepper. Fit the cod fillets into the tin, spooning some of the tomato mixture over the fish, then scatter the prosciutto on top.

2 Roast in a preheated oven, 220°C (425°F), Gas Mark 7, for 15 minutes. Remove the tin from the oven, drizzle over the lemon juice, cover with foil and leave to rest for 5 minutes.

3 Serve the cod by itself or with new potatoes and a green salad, if you like.

serves **4**
preparation time **10 minutes**
cooking time **about 8 minutes**

Grilled salmon
with a chilli crust

**3 teaspoons crushed dried
 red chillies**
3 tablespoons sesame seeds
**1 large bunch of flat leaf
 parsley, chopped**
**4 salmon fillets, about 150 g
 (5 oz) each, skinned**
1 egg white, lightly beaten
**salt and freshly ground black
 pepper**

to serve
1 lime, halved
noodles (optional)

1 Heat a ridged griddle pan over a medium heat. Combine the chillies, sesame seeds, parsley and salt and pepper on a plate.

2 Dip the salmon fillets into the egg white, then into the chilli mixture to coat. Pat the mixture on to the salmon to ensure an even coating.

3 Put the salmon fillets into the hot pan and cook for 4 minutes on each side, turning them carefully with a spatula and keeping the crust on the fish. Add the lime halves, cut side down, to the pan for the last 2 minutes of the cooking time and cook until charred. Serve the salmon with the lime halves and with noodles, if you like.

FAST FOOD TIP
The chilli crust not only looks good, but it also imparts some delicious flavours to the fish.

serves **4**
preparation time **5 minutes**
cooking time **about 12 minutes**

Five-spice salmon
with Asian greens

**2 teaspoons crushed black
  peppercorns**
**2 teaspoons Chinese
  five-spice powder**
1 teaspoon salt
¼ teaspoon cayenne pepper
**4 salmon fillets, about 200 g
  (7 oz) each, skinned**
3 tablespoons sunflower oil
**500 g (1 lb) choi sum or pak
  choi, sliced**
3 garlic cloves, sliced
**3 tablespoons Shao Hsing
  wine or dry sherry**
75 ml (3 fl oz) vegetable stock
2 tablespoons light soy sauce
1 teaspoon sesame oil
plain boiled rice, to serve

1 Heat a ridged griddle pan over a medium heat. Combine the pepper, five-spice powder, salt and cayenne on a plate. Brush the salmon fillets with a little of the sunflower oil and dip them into the spice mixture to coat.

2 Put the salmon fillets into the hot pan and cook for 4 minutes, then turn and cook for a further 2–3 minutes until the fish is just cooked through. Transfer to a plate, cover with foil and leave to rest for 5 minutes.

3 Meanwhile, heat the remaining oil in a wok over a high heat and stir-fry the greens for 2 minutes. Add the garlic and stir-fry for a further minute.

4 Add the wine or sherry, stock, soy sauce and sesame oil and cook for a further 2 minutes until the greens are tender. Serve the salmon and greens with a bowl of boiled rice.

FAST FOOD TIP
Chinese five-spice powder is a ready-made blend of Szechuan peppercorns, cassia or cinnamon, cloves, fennel seeds and star anise, and gives this dish an unmistakable Asian flavour. Shao Hsing is a Chinese rice wine, which is available from specialist Chinese food stores, but you can use dry sherry or another rice wine as an alternative.

serves **4**
preparation time **10 minutes**
cooking time **15 minutes**

Grilled snapper
with carrots and caraway seeds

500 g (1 lb) carrots, sliced
2 teaspoons caraway seeds
4 snapper fillets, about 175 g
(6 oz) each
2 oranges
1 bunch of fresh coriander,
roughly chopped, plus extra
to garnish
50 ml (2 fl oz) olive oil
salt and freshly ground black
pepper

1 Heat a ridged griddle pan over a medium heat. Put the carrots into the pan and cook for 3 minutes on each side, adding the caraway seeds for the last 2 minutes of the cooking time. Transfer to a bowl and keep warm.

2 Put the snapper fillets into the pan and cook for 3 minutes on each side.

3 Meanwhile, juice one of the oranges and cut the other into quarters. Put the orange quarters into the pan and cook until browned.

4 Add the coriander to the carrots and mix well. Season with salt and pepper and stir in the oil and orange juice.

5 Serve the cooked fish with the carrots and orange wedges, and garnish with extra chopped coriander.

serves **4**
preparation time **10 minutes**
cooking time **12 minutes**

Thai fishcakes
with sweet chilli sauce

250 g (8 oz) raw tiger prawns, peeled and deveined
250 g (8 oz) skinned white fish fillet, diced
4 fresh kaffir lime leaves, very finely chopped
4 spring onions, trimmed and finely chopped
2 tablespoons chopped fresh coriander
1 small egg, beaten
2 tablespoons Thai fish sauce
65 g (2½ oz) rice flour
sunflower oil, for shallow-frying
lime wedges, to garnish
sweet chilli sauce, to serve

1 Put all the ingredients, except the oil, into a food processor and pulse briefly until well blended. Use wet hands to shape the mixture into 12 flat cakes about 5 cm (2 inches) across.

2 Heat 1 cm (½ inch) of oil in a frying pan and fry the cakes in batches for 2 minutes on each side until golden. Drain on kitchen paper and keep warm in a low oven while cooking the remainder.

3 Garnish the fishcakes with lime wedges and serve with sweet chilli sauce for dipping.

FAST FOOD TIP
You can use any firm white fish, such as haddock, cod or ling, to make these delicious fishcakes. The mixture will be slightly sticky once all the ingredients are blended, so wet your hands with cold water before shaping it into the cakes.

serves **2**
preparation time **10 minutes, plus marinating**
cooking time **4 minutes**

Lime, coconut
and chilli-spiked squid

10–12 prepared baby squid, about 375 g (12 oz) in total including tentacles
4 limes, halved
mixed green salad, to serve

dressing
2 red chillies, deseeded and finely chopped
juice and grated rind of 2 limes
2.5 cm (1 inch) piece of fresh root ginger, peeled and grated
50 g (2 oz) dried, creamed or freshly grated coconut
50 ml (2 fl oz) groundnut oil
1–2 tablespoons chilli oil
1 tablespoon white wine vinegar

1 Cut open each squid tube lengthways to form a flat sheet. Using a sharp knife, score the inside flesh lightly in a crisscross pattern.

2 Mix all the dressing ingredients together in a bowl, then pour half into a separate bowl. Toss the squid in half the dressing, cover and leave to marinate in the refrigerator for about 1 hour. Reserve the remaining dressing.

3 Heat a ridged griddle pan over a high heat. Put the limes, cut side down, into the pan and cook for about 2 minutes until nicely charred. Set aside.

4 Keeping the griddle pan very hot, add the squid to the pan and cook quickly for 1 minute. Turn them over and cook for a further minute until charred.

5 Place the squid on a chopping board and cut them into strips. Transfer to serving plates, top with the remaining dressing and serve with the limes and a mixed green salad.

FAST FOOD TIP
If you don't have time to marinate the squid, just toss the pieces in the dressing before cooking and drizzle more over them before serving. Be careful not to overcook the squid, because they will quickly turn rubbery in texture and taste unpleasant.

serves **2**
preparation time **15 minutes**
cooking time **5 minutes**

Seared scallops
with coriander yogurt

150 ml (¼ pint) natural soya yogurt
2 tablespoons chopped fresh coriander
finely grated rind and juice of 1 lime
2 teaspoons sesame oil
½ small red onion, finely chopped
15 g (½ oz) fresh root ginger, peeled and grated
1 garlic clove, crushed
2 teaspoons caster sugar
2 teaspoons dark soy sauce
1 tablespoon water
1 pointed green pepper, cored, deseeded and thinly sliced
12 large fresh scallops, shelled and cleaned
rocket leaves, to serve

1 Mix the yogurt with the coriander and lime rind in a small bowl, then transfer to a serving dish.

2 To make the soy glaze, heat half the oil in a small saucepan and gently fry the onion for 3 minutes until softened. Remove the pan from the heat and add the ginger, garlic, sugar, soy sauce, water and lime juice.

3 Brush a frying pan with the remaining oil. Add the green pepper and scallops and cook the scallops for 1 minute on each side until cooked through. Cook the pepper for a little longer if necessary.

4 Pile the pepper and scallops on to serving plates with the rocket leaves. Heat the soy glaze through and spoon it over the scallops. Serve with the yogurt sauce.

FAST FOOD TIP
To turn this dish into a starter for 4, just serve 3 scallops per portion.

serves **4**
preparation time **15 minutes**
cooking time **15 minutes**

Mussel and lemon curry

1 kg (2 lb) live mussels,
   scrubbed and debearded
100 ml (3½ fl oz) lager
100 g (3½ oz) unsalted butter
1 onion, chopped
1 garlic clove, crushed
2.5 cm (1 inch) piece of
   fresh root ginger, peeled
   and grated
1 tablespoon medium curry
   powder
150 ml (¼ pint) single cream
2 tablespoons lemon juice
salt and freshly ground black
   pepper
chopped flat leaf parsley, to
   garnish
crusty bread, to serve
   (optional)

1 Discard any mussels that are broken or do not close
immediately when sharply tapped with a knife. Put them into
a large saucepan with the lager, cover and cook, shaking the
pan frequently, for 4 minutes until all the shells have opened.
Discard any that remain closed. Strain, reserve the cooking
liquid and keep it warm.

2 Melt the butter in a large saucepan and fry the onion,
garlic, ginger and curry powder, stirring frequently, for
5 minutes. Strain in the reserved cooking liquid, bring to the
boil and boil until reduced by half. Whisk in the cream and
lemon juice and simmer gently.

3 Stir the mussels into the sauce and warm through, then
season with salt and pepper. Garnish with chopped parsley
and serve with crusty bread, if you like.

Vegetarian

Pasta is a quick and easy meat-free favourite, and this rendition is redolent with herbs. Ready-made bases also make homemade pizzas a fast food option, here featuring speciality cheeses. And adaptable tofu stars in fruity bangers and spicy burgers.

serves **4**
preparation time **5 minutes**
cooking time **15–20 minutes**

Roasted cherry tomato
and ricotta pasta

500 g (1 lb) cherry tomatoes,
    halved
4 tablespoons extra virgin
    olive oil
2 teaspoons chopped thyme
4 garlic cloves, sliced
pinch of dried red chilli flakes
400 g (13 oz) dried pasta
1 bunch of basil leaves, torn
125 g (4 oz) ricotta cheese,
    crumbled
salt and freshly ground black
    pepper

1 Put the tomatoes into a roasting tin with the oil, thyme, garlic and chilli flakes, and season with salt and pepper. Cook in a preheated oven, 200ºC (400ºF), Gas Mark 6, for 15–20 minutes until the tomatoes have softened and released their juices.

2 Meanwhile, cook the pasta in a saucepan of lightly salted boiling water for 10–12 minutes or according to the packet instructions. Drain and return to the pan.

3 Stir the tomatoes with their pan juices and most of the basil leaves into the cooked pasta and toss gently until combined. Season with salt and pepper and spoon into bowls. Chop the remaining basil, mix into the ricotta, season with salt and pepper and spoon into a small dish for guests to spoon on to the pasta.

FAST FOOD TIP
This piquant, herb-scented dish can be made with just about any shape or variety of pasta you like. Always check the packet for cooking instructions because cooking times will vary.

serves **4**
preparation time **5 minutes**
cooking time **10 minutes**

Asparagus and taleggio pizza

**5 tablespoons passata
(sieved tomatoes)**
**1 tablespoon ready-made
red pesto**
**4 x 25 cm (10 inch) ready-
made pizza bases**
**250 g (8 oz) taleggio cheese,
derinded and sliced**
**175 g (6 oz) slim asparagus
spears, trimmed**
2 tablespoons olive oil
**salt and freshly ground
black pepper**

1 Mix the passata with the pesto and a pinch of salt and spread over the pizza bases. Top with the taleggio and asparagus and drizzle with the oil.

2 Place the pizzas directly on the shelves of a preheated oven, 200ºC (400ºF), Gas Mark 6, and bake for 10 minutes until the asparagus is tender and the pizza bases are crisp. Grind over some pepper before serving.

FAST FOOD TIP
Taleggio is a soft and creamy Italian cheese with a slightly sweet flavour and rich, creamy texture that melts perfectly on top of the pizza. Look out for slim asparagus that will roast quickly. If you can only find large stalks, halve them lengthways before scattering over the pizza.

serves **4**
preparation time **10 minutes**
cooking time **16 minutes**

Thai coconut greens
with soba

1 tablespoon sunflower oil
1 onion, chopped
4 teaspoons Thai red curry
  paste
400 ml (14 fl oz) can reduced-
  fat coconut milk
150 ml (¼ pint) vegetable
  stock
1 carrot, cut into matchstick
  strips
100 g (3½ oz) purple
  sprouting broccoli
125 g (4 oz) pak choi
1 small bunch of fresh
  coriander
100 g (3½ oz) green beans,
  thickly sliced
200 g (7 oz) soba (Japanese
  noodles)
75 g (3 oz) frozen peas
  (optional)
50 g (2 oz) dry-roasted
  unsalted peanuts

1 Heat the oil in a saucepan and fry the onion for 5 minutes until softened.

2 Stir in the curry paste and cook for 1 minute, then stir in the coconut milk and stock and add the carrot strips. Cover and simmer for 5 minutes.

3 Meanwhile, thickly slice the broccoli stems and halve the florets. Cut the leaves from the pak choi and shred. Cut the white stems into matchstick strips. Reserve some coriander for a garnish, then roughly chop the rest.

4 Add the green beans and broccoli stems to the pan, cover again and cook for 3 minutes. Half-fill a separate saucepan with water and bring to the boil, then add the soba. Simmer for 3–5 minutes until just cooked, then drain.

5 Add the broccoli florets, pak choi strips and leaves and the peas, if using, to the curry and cook for 2 minutes.

6 Spoon the soba into mounds in 4 shallow dishes. Stir the chopped coriander into the curry, then spoon the curry on top of the soba and pour the sauce into the base of the dish. Garnish with the peanuts and the reserved coriander.

serves **4**
preparation time **5 minutes**
cooking time **10–12 minutes**

Gnocchi with spinach
and three-cheese sauce

500 g (1 lb) ready-made gnocchi
250 g (8 oz) frozen leaf spinach, thawed
250 g (8 oz) mascarpone cheese
50 g (2 oz) dolcelatte cheese
pinch of grated nutmeg
2 tablespoons freshly grated Parmesan cheese
salt and freshly ground black pepper

1 Cook the gnocchi in a saucepan of lightly salted boiling water according to the packet instructions. Drain well and return them to the pan.

2 Meanwhile, drain the spinach, use your hands to squeeze out all the excess water and roughly chop. Stir the spinach into the cooked gnocchi with the mascarpone, dolcelatte and nutmeg. Stir gently until creamy, then season with salt and pepper.

3 Spoon the gnocchi mixture into a shallow heatproof dish, sprinkle over the Parmesan and cook under a preheated hot grill for 5–6 minutes until bubbling and golden. Serve the gnocchi immediately.

FAST FOOD TIP
Ready-made gnocchi make a great alternative to pasta. For a special occasion, you could divide the little potato dumplings and the spinach and cheese sauce between individual gratin dishes and grill for 3–4 minutes until golden and bubbling.

serves **4**
preparation time **20 minutes**
cooking time **10 minutes**

Smoked tofu
and apricot sausages

**225 g (7½ oz) smoked firm
  tofu**
**2 tablespoons olive or soya
  oil, plus a little extra for
  shallow-frying**
**1 large onion, roughly
  chopped**
**2 celery sticks, roughly
  chopped**
**100 g (3½ oz) ready-to-eat
  dried apricots, roughly
  chopped**
50 g (2 oz) breadcrumbs
1 egg
1 tablespoon chopped sage
**salt and freshly ground black
  pepper**

to serve
chunky chips
spicy relish

1 Pat the tofu dry on kitchen paper and tear into chunks. Heat the oil in a frying pan and fry the onion and celery for 5 minutes until softened. Tip them into a food processor, add the tofu and apricots and whiz to a chunky paste, scraping down the mixture from the sides of the bowl if necessary.

2 Tip the mixture into a mixing bowl and add the breadcrumbs, egg and sage. Season with salt and pepper and beat well until everything is evenly combined.

3 Divide the mixture into 8 portions. Using lightly floured hands, shape each portion into a sausage, pressing the mixture together firmly. Heat a little oil in a frying pan, preferably nonstick, and fry the sausages for about 5 minutes until golden. Serve with chunky chips and relish.

FAST FOOD TIP
This quantity makes 8 small sausages, so you might want to make double the quantity for people with larger appetites.

serves **4**
preparation time **10 minutes**
cooking time **about 15 minutes**

Mediterranean goats'
cheese omelette

4 tablespoons extra virgin
    olive oil
500 g (1 lb) cherry tomatoes,
    halved
a little chopped basil, plus
    extra sprigs to garnish
12 eggs
2 tablespoons wholegrain
    mustard
50 g (2 oz) butter
100 g (3½ oz) soft goats'
    cheese, diced
salt and freshly ground black
    pepper
watercress, to garnish

1 Heat the oil in a frying pan and fry the tomatoes (you may have to do this in 2 batches) for 2–3 minutes until softened. Add the chopped basil, season with salt and pepper, transfer to a bowl and keep warm.

2 Beat the eggs with the mustard and season with salt and pepper. Melt a quarter of the butter in an omelette or small frying pan until it stops foaming, then swirl in a quarter of the egg mixture. Fork over the omelette so that it cooks evenly.

3 As soon as it is set on the bottom (but still a little runny in the middle), dot over a quarter of the goats' cheese and cook for a further 30 seconds. Carefully slide the omelette on to a warmed serving plate, folding it in half as you go. Keep warm while cooking the remaining omelettes.

4 Repeat with the remaining butter, egg mixture and cheese to make 3 more omelettes. Serve them with the tomatoes and garnish with watercress and basil sprigs.

FAST FOOD TIP
It's a good idea to use a combination of red and yellow cherry tomatoes for maximum colour impact.

serves **4**
preparation time **5 minutes**
cooking time **7–8 minutes**

Flatbread pizza
with tomatoes and goats' cheese

4 x 20 cm (8 inch)
   Mediterranean flatbreads
2 tablespoons sun-dried
   tomato paste
300 g (10 oz) mozzarella
   cheese, sliced
6 plum tomatoes, roughly
   chopped
4 tablespoons olive oil
1 garlic clove, crushed
small handful of basil leaves,
   roughly torn
100 g (3½ oz) goats' cheese
salt and freshly ground black
   pepper

1 Place the flatbreads on 2 baking sheets and spread with the sun-dried tomato paste. Top with the sliced mozzarella and bake in a preheated oven, 200°C (400°F), Gas Mark 6, for 7–8 minutes until the bases are crisp and the cheese has melted.

2 Meanwhile, put the plum tomatoes into a bowl, add the oil, garlic and basil and season generously with salt and pepper.

3 Top the cooked pizza with the tomatoes and crumble over the goats' cheese. Serve immediately.

FAST FOOD TIP
Mediterranean flatbreads crisp up beautifully in the oven or under the grill, making them a perfect alternative to the classic pizza base.

serves **2**
preparation time **10 minutes**
cooking time **12 minutes**

Devilled tofu
and mushrooms

½ **teaspoon cornflour**
juice of 1 large orange
2 tablespoons mango
    chutney
2 tablespoons
    Worcestershire sauce
1 tablespoon grainy mustard
125 g (4 oz) firm tofu
40 g (1½ oz) butter
375 g (12 oz) large open
    mushrooms
2 chunky slices of wholegrain
    bread, toasted
salt and freshly ground
    black pepper
chopped flat leaf parsley, to
    garnish

1 Blend the cornflour with a little of the orange juice in a small bowl until smooth. Add the chutney to the bowl, chopping up any large pieces, together with the Worcestershire sauce, mustard and the remaining orange juice.

2 Pat the tofu dry on kitchen paper and cut it into 1 cm (½ inch) dice. Melt the butter in a frying pan and fry the tofu for 3–5 minutes, turning it frequently, until golden, then drain it. Fry the mushrooms in the pan for 5 minutes.

3 Return the tofu to the pan with the orange sauce and cook gently for 2 minutes, stirring, until the sauce is slightly thickened and bubbling. Season with salt and pepper, spoon it over the hot toast and garnish with chopped parsley.

FAST FOOD TIP
Use a chunky, grainy bread for the toast so that it absorbs all the sweet and spicy devilled sauce.

serves **4**
preparation time **15 minutes**
cooking time **15 minutes**

Spicy tofu burgers
with cucumber relish

**4 tablespoons soya or
 groundnut oil**
**1 small red onion, finely
 chopped**
1 celery stick, finely chopped
2 garlic cloves, crushed
**200 g (7 oz) can red kidney
 beans, drained and rinsed**
75 g (3 oz) salted peanuts
250 g (8 oz) firm tofu
**2 teaspoons medium
 curry paste**
50 g (2 oz) breadcrumbs
1 egg
**½ small cucumber, peeled and
 deseeded**
**2 tablespoons chopped flat
 leaf parsley**
**1 tablespoon white wine
 vinegar**
2 teaspoons caster sugar

to serve
hamburger buns or bread rolls
lettuce leaves

1 Heat 1 tablespoon of the oil in a frying pan and gently fry all but 1 tablespoon of the onion with the celery for 5 minutes until softened. Add the garlic and fry for a further 2 minutes.

2 Put the beans into a bowl and mash them lightly with a fork to break them up. Finely chop the peanuts in a food processor. Pat the tofu dry on kitchen paper, break it into pieces and add it to the nuts in the food processor. Whiz until the tofu is crumbly, then add the mixture to the beans together with the fried vegetables, curry paste, breadcrumbs and egg and mix everything well to obtain a thick paste.

3 Divide the mixture into quarters and shape into burgers, dusting your hands with flour if the mixture is sticky. Heat the remaining oil in the pan and gently fry the burgers for about 4 minutes on each side until golden. Drain on kitchen paper.

4 Meanwhile, chop the cucumber finely and mix it with the reserved tablespoon of chopped onion, the parsley, vinegar and sugar in a small bowl. Serve each burger in a hamburger bun or bread roll with lettuce, topped with the relish.

> **FAST FOOD TIP**
> Red kidney beans add colour and texture to these chunky burgers, but other cooked beans, such as soya beans, would work in this dish just as well.

Desserts

These desserts are simple, sumptuous and healthy. Refreshing iced delights feature citrus fruits and mango, while sweet berries and spiced rhubarb flavour chilled set puddings. And even warm mini tarts involve minimal fat as well as effort.

serves **4**
preparation time **10–15 minutes, plus cooling and freezing**
cooking time **10 minutes**

Lemon yogurt ice

175 g (6 oz) caster sugar
150 ml (¼ pint) water
finely grated rind and juice
  of 2 large lemons
500 ml (17 fl oz) natural
  soya yogurt

1 Put the sugar and water into a large saucepan and heat gently, stirring, until the sugar has dissolved. Leave to cool.

2 Whisk in the lemon rind, juice and yogurt until the mixture is very smooth.

3 To freeze by hand, pour the mixture into a shallow freezer container and freeze for 3–4 hours until frozen around the edges and slushy in the centre. Turn the mixture into a bowl and whisk with an electric whisk until smooth. Return it to the container and re-freeze until softly frozen. Repeat the freezing and whisking process until the yogurt ice has a creamy consistency.

4 To freeze using an ice-cream maker, churn until the mixture is thick and creamy, then transfer to a freezer container and freeze.

5 Transfer the yogurt ice to the refrigerator to soften slightly about 30 minutes before serving.

FAST FOOD TIP
Serve this as a lighter, more refreshing alternative to ice cream or as a long, cooling summer drink, scooped into glasses and topped up with lemonade.

Pink grapefruit parfait

2 pink grapefruits
5 tablespoons dark
muscovado sugar, plus
extra for sprinkling
225 ml (7½ fl oz) double
cream
150 ml (¼ pint) natural yogurt
3 tablespoons elderflower
cordial
½ teaspoon ground ginger
½ teaspoon ground cinnamon
brandy snaps, to serve
(optional)

1 Finely grate the rind of 1 grapefruit, making sure you don't get any of the bitter white pith. Cut the skin and white pith off both grapefruits and cut between each membrane to remove the segments. Put into a large dish, sprinkle with 2 tablespoons of the sugar and set aside.

2 Whisk the cream with the yogurt in a large bowl until thick but not stiff. Fold in the elderflower cordial, spices, grapefruit rind and remaining sugar until smooth.

3 Pour the mixture into attractive glasses, arranging the grapefruit segments between layers of parfait. Sprinkle the top with sugar and serve immediately with brandy snaps, if you like.

FAST FOOD TIP
This recipe also works really well with orange segments and chocolate shavings instead of grapefruit and ginger.

serves **6**

preparation time **15 minutes, plus chilling**

cooking time **4–5 minutes**

Red berry terrine

450 ml (¾ pint) unsweetened
  red grape juice
2 x 15 g (½ oz) sachets
  powdered gelatine
50 g (2 oz) caster sugar
500 g (1 lb) bag frozen mixed
  berry fruits, plus a few extra
  thawed or fresh fruits
  to decorate (optional)

1 Measure 150 ml (¼ pint) of the grape juice into a heatproof bowl and sprinkle over the gelatine, making sure that all the powder has been absorbed by the juice. Leave to stand for 5 minutes.

2 Stand the bowl in a saucepan of simmering water and heat gently for 4–5 minutes until the gelatine has completely dissolved.

3 Stir the sugar into the gelatine mixture, then mix with the remaining grape juice.

4 Pour the still-frozen fruits into a 1 kg (2 lb) loaf tin and cover with the warm juice mixture. Mix to combine, then chill in the refrigerator for 3 hours until set and the fruits have fully thawed.

5 To serve, dip the loaf tin into a bowl of just-boiled water. Count to 10, then loosen the edge of the jelly and turn out on to a serving plate. Decorate with a few extra fruits if you like and serve the jelly cut into thick slices.

FAST FOOD TIP
This is a fresh fruity dessert that is high in vitamins and low in calories.

serves **4**
preparation time **25 minutes, plus freezing**
cooking time **4–5 minutes**

Lime and mango granita

50 g (2 oz) caster sugar
300 ml (½ pint) water
finely grated rind and juice
of 2 limes
1 large ripe mango, plus extra
slices to serve
lime rind curls, to decorate

1 Put the sugar, water and lime rind into a small saucepan and heat gently for 4–5 minutes until the sugar has completely dissolved. Leave to cool.

2 Cut a thick slice off either side of the mango to reveal the large, flat stone, then make crisscross cuts in these slices and scoop the flesh away from the skin using a spoon. Cut away the flesh surrounding the stone and remove and discard the skin. Purée the mango flesh in a blender or food processor until smooth, or rub through a sieve.

3 Mix the mango purée with the sugar syrup and lime juice, then pour into a shallow roasting tin so that it is about 2 cm (¾ inch) deep. Freeze for 1 hour.

4 Take the tin out of the freezer and mash the mixture with a fork to break up any large ice crystals. Return to the freezer and freeze for 1½ hours, beating with a fork at 30-minute intervals until the granita has the consistency of crushed ice.

5 Spoon into 4 dishes, decorate with the lime rind curls and serve with extra slices of mango. Transfer any remaining granita to a plastic freezer container with a lid and return to the freezer.

> **FAST FOOD TIP**
> Light, tangy and refreshing, this is the perfect dessert to follow a spicy curry or chilli.

serves **4**
preparation time **5 minutes**
cooking time **7–10 minutes**

Cherry and cinnamon zabaglione

4 egg yolks
125 g (4 oz) caster sugar
150 ml (¼ pint) cream sherry
large pinch of ground
** cinnamon**
425 g (14 oz) can black
** cherries in syrup**
2 amaretti biscuits, crumbled,
** to decorate**

1 Pour 5 cm (2 inches) of water into a medium saucepan and bring to the boil. Cover with a large heatproof bowl, making sure that the water does not touch the base of the bowl.

2 Reduce the heat so that the water is simmering, then add the egg yolks, sugar, sherry and cinnamon to the bowl. Whisk for 5–8 minutes until very thick and foamy and the custard leaves a trail when the whisk is lifted above the mixture.

3 Drain off some of the cherry syrup, then tip the cherries and just a little of the syrup into a small saucepan. Warm through, then spoon into 4 glasses. Pour the warm zabaglione over the top and decorate with crumbled amaretti biscuits. Serve immediately.

FAST FOOD TIP
Measure out the ingredients before you sit down to your main course so that you can whip up this dessert in a matter of moments.

serves **4**
preparation time **5 minutes**
cooking time **8 minutes**

Figs
with yogurt and honey

8 ripe figs
4 tablespoons natural yogurt
2 tablespoons clear honey

1 Heat a frying pan over a medium heat and add the figs. Cook for 8 minutes, turning occasionally, until they are charred on the outside. Remove and cut in half.

2 Arrange the figs on 4 plates and serve with a spoonful of yogurt and some honey drizzled over the top.

FAST FOOD TIP
Buy figs when they are in season and full of flavour and juice.

serves **4**
preparation time **10 minutes**
cooking time **12 minutes**

Drunken orange slices

4 large sweet oranges
50 ml (2 fl oz) cold water
50 g (2 oz) soft brown sugar
3 tablespoons Cointreau
2 tablespoons whisky
juice of 1 small orange
1 vanilla pod, split
1 cinnamon stick
4 cloves
2–3 mace blades (optional)
ginger or other ice cream,
    to serve

1 Using a small, sharp knife, cut off the base and the top of each orange. Cut down around the curve of the orange to remove all the peel and pith, leaving just the orange flesh. Cut the flesh horizontally into 5 mm (¼ inch) slices and set aside.

2 Put the water, sugar, 2 tablespoons of the Cointreau, the whisky, orange juice, vanilla pod, cinnamon stick, cloves and mace, if using, into a small saucepan and heat gently until the sugar has dissolved. Increase the heat and boil rapidly for 5 minutes. Leave to cool slightly, but keep warm.

3 Heat a griddle pan over a high heat. Put the orange slices into the pan and cook for 1 minute on each side until caramelized. Top with the remaining Cointreau and set alight. Once the flames have died down, arrange the orange slices on serving dishes and drizzle with the syrup.

4 Serve the orange slices immediately with the ginger ice cream or an ice cream of your choice.

serves **4**
preparation time **15 minutes, plus cooling**
cooking time **5 minutes**

Papaya
and lime salad

3 firm ripe papayas
2 limes
**2 teaspoons soft brown
  sugar**
**75 g (3 oz) blanched almonds,
  toasted**
lime wedges, to garnish

1 Cut the papayas in half, scoop out the seeds and discard. Peel the halves, cut the flesh roughly into dice and put into a bowl. Finely grate the rind of both limes, then squeeze 1 of the limes and reserve the juice. Cut the pith off the second lime and, holding it over the bowl of diced papaya to catch the juice, cut between each membrane to remove the segments. Add the lime segments and grated rind to the papaya.

2 Pour the lime juice into a small saucepan, add the sugar and heat gently until the sugar has dissolved. Remove from the heat and leave to cool.

3 When the sweetened lime juice has cooled, pour it over the fruit and toss thoroughly. Add the toasted almonds to the fruit salad and serve, garnished with lime wedges.

FAST FOOD TIP
This simple but utterly delicious fruit salad can also be served for brunch or breakfast with muesli and yogurt, or on its own.

serves **4**
preparation time **10 minutes**
cooking time **4–5 minutes for each waffle**

Waffles
with summer berry compote

150 g (5 oz) strawberries, hulled and quartered
150 g (5 oz) raspberries
150 g (5 oz) blueberries
2 tablespoons elderflower cordial
4 tablespoons low-fat Greek yogurt, to serve (optional)

waffles
75 g (3 oz) unsalted butter
125 ml (4 fl oz) semi-skimmed milk
2 eggs, separated
125 g (4 oz) self-raising wholemeal flour
2 tablespoons icing sugar, sifted
grated rind of ½ lemon

1 To make the waffles, melt the butter in a small saucepan, then leave to cool a little. Meanwhile, pour the milk into a bowl, add the egg yolks and whisk lightly. Add 1 tablespoon of the melted butter and work in lightly with a fork.

2 Heat a waffle iron on the hob or preheat an electric one while you sift the flour into a separate bowl. Make a well in the centre of the flour and gradually beat in the milk mixture and the remaining butter. Whisk the egg whites in a large bowl until stiff enough to hold firm peaks, then fold into the batter with the icing sugar and the lemon rind.

3 Grease the waffle iron and pour in about one-eighth of the batter. Close the lid and cook for 4–5 minutes, turning the iron once or twice if using a hob model. When the waffle is golden brown and cooked, remove from the iron, cover and keep warm while cooking the remaining waffles.

4 Meanwhile, put all the berries and the elderflower cordial into a small saucepan and heat gently until the berries are just starting to release their juice.

5 Put 2 waffles on each plate and serve with the berries and a spoonful of Greek yogurt, if liked

serves **4**
preparation time **10 minutes**
cooking time **6 minutes**

Pancake stack
with maple syrup

1 egg
75 g (3 oz) plain flour
100 ml (3½ fl oz) milk
2½ tablespoons
**   vegetable oil**
1 tablespoon caster sugar
bottled maple syrup, for
**   drizzling**
8 scoops of vanilla ice cream,
**   to serve**

1 To make the pancake batter, put the egg, flour, milk, oil and sugar into a blender or food processor and whiz until smooth and creamy.

2 Heat a frying pan over a medium heat and pour a ladleful of the batter into each corner, to make 4 pancakes. After about 1 minute, the tops of the pancakes will start to set and air bubbles will rise to the top and burst. Using a spatula, turn the pancakes over and cook on the other side for 1 minute.

3 Repeat twice more until you have used all the batter – making 12 small pancakes in all. Bring to the table as a stack, drizzled with maple syrup. Serve 3 pancakes to each person, with 2 scoops of ice cream.

serves **4**
preparation time **15 minutes**

Strawberry and lavender crush

400 g (13 oz) strawberries
2 tablespoons icing sugar,
   plus extra to decorate
4–5 lavender flowers, plus
   extra to decorate
400 g (13 oz) Greek yogurt
4 ready-made meringue nests

1 Reserve 4 small strawberries for decoration. Hull and mash the remainder with the sugar, using a fork or in a blender or food processor. Pull off the lavender flowers from the stems and crumble them into the strawberries to taste.

2 Put the yogurt into a bowl and crumble in the meringues, then lightly mix. Add the strawberry mixture, fold together with a spoon until marbled, then spoon into glasses.

3 Cut the reserved strawberries in half, then decorate the desserts with the strawberry halves and lavender flowers. Dust lightly with icing sugar and serve immediately.

FAST FOOD TIP
If you don't have fresh lavender at home, buy a small pot from a garden centre or use a few dried flowers instead.

serves **12**
preparation time **15 minutes**
cooking time **6–8 minutes**

Mini nectarine
and blueberry tarts

25 g (1 oz) butter, melted
2 teaspoons olive oil
4 sheets of filo pastry, thawed
if frozen, each
30 x 18 cm (12 x 7 inches),
or 65 g (2½ oz) total weight
2 tablespoons reduced-sugar
red berry jam
juice of ½ orange
4 ripe nectarines, halved,
stoned and sliced
150 g (5 oz) blueberries
sifted icing sugar, to decorate
fromage frais or yogurt ice
cream, to serve

1 Heat the butter and oil in a small saucepan until the butter has melted.

2 Unroll the pastry and separate into sheets. Brush lightly with the butter mixture, then cut into 24 pieces, each 10 x 8 cm (4 x 3½ inches).

3 Arrange a piece of filo in each of the sections of a deep 12-hole muffin tin, then add a second piece at a slight angle to the first to give a pretty jagged edge to each pastry case.

4 Bake in a preheated oven, 180°C (350°F), Gas Mark 4, for 6–8 minutes until golden. Meanwhile, warm the jam and orange juice in a saucepan, then add the nectarines and blueberries and warm through.

5 Carefully lift the tart cases out of the muffin tin and transfer to a serving dish. Fill with the warm fruits and dust with sifted icing sugar. Serve with spoonfuls of fromage frais or yogurt ice cream.

> **FAST FOOD TIP**
> These dainty little tarts are made with wafer-thin pieces of filo pastry brushed lightly with melted butter and oil and baked until golden. Even with the addition of melted butter, these tarts are much lower in fat than ones made with shortcrust pastry.

serves **6**
preparation time **20 minutes, plus cooling and chilling**
cooking time **5 minutes**

Vanilla panna cotta
with rhubarb compote

750 g (1½ lb) rhubarb, trimmed and cut into 1.5 cm (¾ inch) lengths
275 g (9 oz) caster sugar
2 cinnamon sticks
3 tablespoons water
1 teaspoon powdered gelatine or vegetarian gelling agent
350 g (11½ oz) silken tofu
250 g (8 oz) mascarpone cheese
1 teaspoon vanilla extract
150 ml (¼ pint) double cream

1 Lightly oil 6 small dariole moulds or 150 ml (¼ pint) metal pudding moulds. Put the rhubarb into a heavy-based saucepan with 175 g (6 oz) of the sugar, the cinnamon sticks and 1 tablespoon of the water. Heat gently, stirring, until the sugar has dissolved. Cover and simmer gently for 3–4 minutes until the rhubarb is tender but not falling apart. Transfer the compote to a bowl and leave to cool.

2 Sprinkle the gelatine over the remaining water in a small bowl and leave to stand. Put the tofu into a blender or food processor with the remaining sugar and whiz until smooth, scraping it down from the sides of the bowl as necessary.

3 Gently melt the mascarpone in a medium, heavy-based saucepan until it is runny. Stir the soaked gelatine into the cheese until it is completely dissolved. Pour into a bowl and beat in the vanilla, tofu mixture and cream. Divide the mixture between the moulds and chill them for at least 4 hours until set.

4 Carefully loosen the edges of the moulds with a knife and turn the puddings on to serving plates. Serve with the rhubarb compote.

FAST FOOD TIP
For best results use early-season rhubarb, while it is still pink and tender. Mature rhubarb loses its delicate colour and will probably need additional sweetening.

Index

Acknowledgements

Executive Editor Nicky Hill
Project Editor Alice Bowden

Executive Art Editor Karen Sawyer
Design Cobalt id

Picture Researcher Sophie Delpech
Production Controller Nosheen Shan

Octopus Publishing Group Limited/William
Lingwood 12, 13, 15, 16, 17, 20, 22, 24, 25, 27, 32,
33, 34, 37, 39, 42, 47, 50, 51, 52, 54, 56, 58, 62, 63,
65, 66, 67, 69, 70, 71, 72, 75, 79, 83, 85, 87, 90, 96,
97, 98, 100, 103, 104, 113, 114, 115, 120, 123, 124;
/Lis Parsons 28, 36, 40, 41, 92, 93, 101, 105, 107,
110, 111, 119, 125; /Gareth Sambidge 21, 29, 44,
55, 78, 80, 82, 86, 89, 116, 118, 121.